Katharine Allen

The Treatment of Nature in the Poetry of the Roman Republic

Katharine Allen

The Treatment of Nature in the Poetry of the Roman Republic

ISBN/EAN: 9783744776660

Printed in Europe, USA, Canada, Australia, Japan

Cover: Foto ©Thomas Meinert / pixelio.de

More available books at **www.hansebooks.com**

BULLETIN OF THE UNIVERSITY OF WISCONSIN

NO. 28.

PHILOLOGY AND LITERATURE SERIES, VOL. 1, No. 2, PP. 89-219.

THE TREATMENT OF NATURE IN THE POETRY OF THE ROMAN REPUBLIC.

(EXCLUSIVE OF COMEDY.)

BY

KATHARINE ALLEN.

A THESIS SUBMITTED FOR THE DEGREE OF DOCTOR OF PHILOSOPHY,
UNIVERSITY OF WISCONSIN, 1898.

*Published bi-monthly by authority of law with the approval of the Regents
of the University and entered at the post office at
Madison as second-class matter.*

MADISON, WISCONSIN

MAY, 1899

TABLE OF CONTENTS.

ERRATA.

Page 96, line 7, ",Sky " is omitted from headings.

Page 97, line 6, for "*celeris*" read "*celer.*"

Page 120, line 23, heading, for "ght" read "Night."

Page 153, line 33 (also page 154, line 12; page 191, lines 4, 8, 11), for "*Favonus*" read "*Favonius.*"

Page 156, line 21, for "*macriae*" read "*materiae.*"

THE TREATMENT OF NATURE IN THE POETRY OF THE ROMAN REPUBLIC.

INTRODUCTION.

In his introduction to "*Ueber die Empfindung der Natur-schönheit bei den Alten*" (1865), Heinrich Motz expressed the feeling that so much had already been written on this subject by so many scholars, that to add more was "to come with an Iliad after Homer."

If apology was necessary for writing on this general theme thirty years ago, it would seem to be doubly necessary at the present time, for the works dealing with it since the time of Motz have been quite as numerous and as important as those preceding him. Yet these works, like their predecessors, are all of a more or less general character. Even Biese, who in "*die Entwicklung des Naturge-fühls bei den Griechen und Römern*," has treated the whole subject in a manner far more thorough and comprehensive than any one else, cannot, within the limits of one small volume, have exhausted it. Many of his conclusions have been put forward both before and since his time, and in their general statement there can be little difference of opinion. It is in matters of detail that there is still room for work within this field.

A few points may be regarded as settled for Roman literature as a whole:

1. That the Roman wrote less of nature for her own sake than does the modern poet.

2. That the aspects of nature which especially attracted the Roman were not, in all cases, the same as those which most appeal to the modern mind.

3. That certain phases of enjoyment in and feeling for nature, commonly expressed in the poetry of today, are ·more rarely expressed in Roman poetry.

It will be the aim of this paper to investigate in detail, for the poets of a single well-defined period, that of the Roman Republic, how far and in what particulars the foregoing statements are actually true, and to add what new generalizations may be made for this special period of Roman poetry.

In the case of each poet must be studied:

(1.) His method of using each form of nature (sky, sea, mountains, etc.) in illustration, in simile, and in metaphor.

(2.) What aspects of each he represented in addition to what may appear in the foregoing figures — (as calm or stormy sea, green or rugged mountains, etc.).

(3 and 4.) What epithets are used and what figurative expressions, in describing each form of nature (links between 2 and 5).

(5.) To what extent natural objects and forces are endowed with life, or with the attributes of personality, the view of nature which merges on one side in the mythological, on the other in the sympathetic or sentimental conception.

(6.) What type of feeling and appreciation for nature is traceable in the writer's way of using and representing her various forms. Is it merely an appreciation of the utility or non-utility of nature to man implied in such references as "fertile fields," "gold-bearing rivers," "barren mountains"? Is it a sense of her grandeur and mystery such as appears in Byron's:

Roll on, thou deep and dark blue ocean—roll!

Is it a purely aesthetic appreciation of her beauty, such as the artist might feel, such as Tennyson expresses in

The long low dune, and lazy-plunging sea,

and, more elaborately, in the opening lines of *Oenone*. Is it, finally, a sense of sympathy between man and nature,

the endowing of nature with a soul in which the human
soul sees itself reflected?   This last, and most characteris-
tically modern feeling for nature may be shown merely in
the use made of nature to enhance the emotional effect of
a scene, where nature is represented in a mood corresponding with the human mood which the poet wishes to represent, or to call forth in the reader, as when King Arthur
in *The Last Tournament*, returning to his deserted home,
enters its portals

> All in a death-dumb, autumn-dripping gloom.

Or when as Eustace goes to court the gardener's daughter,

> All the land in flowery squares
> Beneath a broad and equal-blowing wind,
> Smelt of the coming summer.

Or this feeling may be more definitely and personally expressed, as in Wordsworth's *Tintern Abbey*.

Of necessity these feelings all merge more or less in each
other, no hard and fast line can be drawn, and analysis
must seem often unduly subjective.   To tell where the personalizing of nature's forces ends and mythology begins is
not always possible; to tell where the personalizing of nature ceases to be purely objective, and where the subjective emotional element of comparison begins is often difficult.   The first step in the development of this feeling for
nature is the noting of external resemblances between the
activities of man and nature.   Nature is illustrated from
man, or man from nature.   Next, nature is herself personalized, her actions and manifestations are described in the
terms of human activity, and, as the last step, nature is endowed with human emotions as well as activities, the human soul places its own impress upon nature and feels that
with it and for it nature can rejoice or grieve.

The meagreness of the remains of much of the early poetry, precludes the possibility of making a profitable study
of the successive development of any one sort, and it is
obviously valueless to try to trace such development,

chronologically, through poetry of so many varieties, tragic, epic, satiric, lyric, didactic, as flourished at one time and another before the Augustan age. That Lucretius shows a deeper feeling for nature than does Lucilius, is in such connection entirely without significance. Each poet must be studied individually, and general characteristics for the Republican period, if there be such, may then be deduced. The line of demarcation between the Republic and the Empire is so distinct, the influence of the times upon the literature so quickly seen in other respects, that this boundary line for the present investigation is more real than is always the case in attempted chronological partitions.

CHAPTER I.

PRE-CICERONIAN PERIOD.*

From a study of the earliest Roman poetry no entirely trustworthy conclusions can be reached. The fragmentary nature of the material, the very small number of the fragments in many cases, the loss of much of the Greek poetry which lay behind the Roman, are responsible for this. By the first of these conditions the value of negative results in particular is lessened; by the second, generalization is often made impossible; owing to the third, the distinction between the truly Roman and the borrowed is difficult.

Introductory

It will be necessary while recognizing all this, however, to treat each poet as if complete and independent, and the fact that different poets do, as a matter of fact, even in their fragmentary condition, show some widely different characteristics, makes the result of such an investigation at any rate interesting, if not entirely reliable from the point of view of statistics.

Five of the earliest Roman poets wrote tragedy, and while most of these wrote other kinds of poetry also, it will be most interesting to consider and compare them as writers of tragedy, so far as this is possible. For this reason, Lucilius, who, chronologically considered, should precede Accius, has been left to follow him.

Roman tragedy probably has less claim to originality than any other branch of Roman literature. To make a

---

*The material furnished by comedy is so insignificant that it has seemed best to omit it, and it is with some hesitancy that Lucilius has been included.

thorough investigation of its relations even to its extant
Greek sources, is outside the scope of this paper, yet some
very general conclusions may be reached as to their mutual
relations, even by a superficial comparison.

In treating the various aspects of nature referred to by
each poet, a uniform order has been maintained for con-
venience's sake, the succession being sky, sea, streams,
mountains, woods, plants, animals. Under each of these
heads are treated in order, figurative use, literal representations, epithets, and figurative representations. In some
writers one or more of these divisions is unrepresented.
A general estimate of the poet's feeling and attitude
toward nature follows the detailed treatment in each case.

1. LIVIUS ANDRONICUS.[1]

One-fifth[2] of the seventy-three fragments of Livius
deal with phenomena of nature. Of these the majority are
found in the tragedies (a proportion of one-third), the sea
being the only form of nature better represented in the
translation of the Odyssey.

The melting of ice in spring is figuratively used:

praestatur laus virtuti, sed multo ocius
verno gelu tabescit (R. Liv. 16).

Sea   The sea appears as a region of dreariness
and desolation, in connection with mountains
and desert places:

celsosque (in) ocris
. . . arvaque putria[3] et mare magnum (R. 32),

and as the cruel enemy of man (B. Liv. 22).[4]

---

[1] Tragedy is cited (by verse) from "*Tragicorum Romanorum Fragmenta*," Ribbeck, 1897 (R). For other works, citations are from the
"*Fragmenta Poetarum Romanorum*," Baehrens, 1886 (B).

[2] Figures for the number and proportions of fragments are in every case
merely approximate.

[3] Cf. B. 18 *arvaque Neptuni*. References to ships occur B. 10; 28; 43.

Its epithets describe size, life, and violence: *altus* (B. 43);
inportunus (unda B. 22); *magnus* (R. 33); *saevos* (B. 22).
Once it is distinctly personalized:

> namque nullum plus corpus macerat humanum
> quamde mare saevom: vires cui sunt magnae,
>   topper
> confringent inportunae undae (B. 22).[4]

Streams
The one extant fragment of the *Andromeda* describes the
flood by which Neptune punished the arro-
gance of Cassiopea:

> confluges ubi conventu campum totum inumigant (R. 18),

and the fountain of Castalia is described with a touch of
picturesqueness:

> quo Castalia per struices saxeas lapsu accidit (R. 37).

Mountains
Mountains are represented only as high, *altus* (R. 31),
celsus (R. 34), and rugged, *ocris* (R. 31; 32; 34;
35). Twice Greek mountains are mentioned
by name: Taenarus (R. 34), and Pelion (R. 35).

Plants
Flos liberi occurs (R. 30).
Vacerra is a term of reproach:

> .   .   .   .   vecorde
> et malefica vacerra   .   .   (B. 33).

Animals
The dolphin playing about the ship is described (R. 5);
the hunting dog (R. 29).
To the dolphin are applied the adjectives
lascivus and *simus;* to the dog *odorisequos.*

Summary
Livius' fragments show no use of nature in illustration or
simile. In the description of the sea (B. 22),
a sense of its life and its power is seen, and
the picturesque charm of the running stream is evident in
R. 37. The fragments are too few to afford material for safe

---

[4] The Greek original is as follows:

> οὐ γὰρ ἔγωγέ τί φημι κακώτερον ἄλλο θαλάσσης
> ἄνδρα γε συγχεῦαι, εἰ καὶ μάλα καρτερὸς εἴη. *Od.* 8, 138.

generalization, yet even from these can be inferred a power
of description better than is usually attributed to Livius.[5]

2. NAEVIUS.

Of the one hundred and eighteen fragments of Naevius,
as in Livius, one-fifth are references to nature. As in
Livius, too, the proportion in the tragedies (one-half) is
much greater than elsewhere, except in the case of the sea.
The only reference to the sky is in the *Lycurgus;*

> iam solis aestu candor cum liquesceret (R. Naev. 48).

and in the *Bellum Punicum* (B. Naev. 25).
The north wind is personified in the *Iphigenia* and called
upon:

> passo velo vicinum, Aquilo, (Orestem) in portum fer foras (R. 16).[6]

The sea is referred to only briefly, and almost always in
connection with ships.[7] Its calm aspect alone
Sea   appears, denoted by *flustris* (B. 51); *liquidus*
(B. 36); *favens* (*fretum* R. 53);[8] the last implying something of personalization.

References to streams are found in four fragments, in
two of which the language is figurative. The
Streams   violence of Lycurgus, in the tragedy of that
name, is compared to a swift stream: *sic quasi amnis celeris
rapit* (R. 39). There is a fountain of gold:

> auri rubeo [9] fonte lavere (me) memini manum (R. 6).

---

[5] Biese, p. 8, says of Livius, "Nur genannt, nicht geschildert werden hohe
Berge, winterliche Gefilde, das grosse Meer und die Kastalie, die über
Steingeklüft hingleitet."

[6] Hardly more than a translation from Euripides:

> ἴτ' ὦ πνοαί, ναυσθλοῦσθε τὸν Ἀγαμέμνονος
> παῖδ' εἰς Ἀθήνας. *Iph. in Tauris*, 1487.

[7] An unimportant reference occurs R. 52.

[8] Assigned by R. to the *Iphigenia*. Cf. Eur. *Iph. in Tauris*, 1388,
εὔξεινον πόρον.

[9] *Nireo* edit. of 1871. The text of the whole passage is very doubtful.

The Ister is mentioned by name (R. 62), and the Strymon is evidently referred to in the description of the Bacchae in the *Lycurgus:*

> namque ludere ut laetantis inter se vidimus
> propter amnem, aquam creterris sumere ex fonte (R. 41).

Streams are described as *celeris* (R. 39); *liquidus* (B. 29).

Mountains Mountains are mentioned only once, and then in the same way as by Livius, *montes confragos* (R. 55) being the equivalent. of *ocres.*[10] Upland regions are also referred to in the expression *altus saltus* (R. 27) in the *Lycurgus.*

ᵣ In the same play are described:

Woods
> *frondiferos*[11] locos,
> ingenio arbusta ubi nata[12] sunt, non obsita (R. 22).

In the *Bellum Punicum* are *silvicolae homines* (B. 23).

Plants *Scopas atque verbenas* (B. 34) are mentioned in connection with religious ceremonies only.

Animals Animals are generally found in comparisons. In the satires is found:

> atque prius pariet bovem lucusta Lucam (B. 62).

In the *Lycurgus* the captured Bacchae are represented:

> (sic) sine ferro pecua manibus (sueta) ut ad mortem meant (R. 44).

and

> ducite
> eo cum argutis linguis mutas quadrupedis (R. 25).

> sublimen altos saltus inlicite invios,
> ubi bipedes volucres lino linquant lumina (R. 27).

iubatos angues are found (R. 18).

Summary Streams and animal life are comparatively well represented. More phases of nature are shown than in Livius, but the descriptions, though more numerous, are on the whole less interesting. Only the most

---

[10] *Ocrem antiqui montem confragosum vocabant* (Fest. 181.)

[11] Where epithets are few and found only in passages quoted, they are italicized, and not quoted separately.

[12] *Vineta*, MSS.

ordinary aspects are shown, either by epithet or otherwise. Color terms are entirely lacking.

The address to the north wind and the description of the Bacchae on the banks of the Strymon show a touch of interest above the rest.

3. ENNIUS.

Of the seven hundred and fifty-eight fragments of Ennius, as in Livius and Naevius, a proportion of about one-fifth describe phenomena of nature. The division between the tragedies and other works, however, is very different. In both Livius and Naevius the proportion of fragments of tragedy dealing with nature is much larger than that of other works. In Ennius the reverse is true; of the tragedies only one-sixth of the fragments are concerned with nature; of the annals and satires together, one-fourth.

The sky is described with all manner of imagery — sometimes uncouth, but often vivid. Once, possibly, it is used in a simile:

Sky

fortis Romani sunt tam quam [13] caelus profundus (B. Enn. 377).

Many characteristics of the sky are shown: *caeli caerula templa* (B. 28. 15; 54); *templa caeli summa* (R. Enn. 372); *caeli plagas* (R. 201); *mundus caeli vastus* (B. 467). Its relation to the gods: *magna templa caelitum* (R. 163); *Plagas caelestum* (B. 511.3); *diuom domus altisonum cael* (B. 360); *templum magnum Iovis altitonantis* (B. 310). Its rounded appearance:[14] *cava caeli* (R. 95); *cava caerula* (R. 251). Its brilliance: *hoc sublimen candens* (R. 302). The night sky with its stars:

caelum suspexit stellis fulgentibus aptum (B. 113), (cf. B. 47).

vertitur interea caelum cum ingentibus signis (B. 150).

and again R. 163, (p. 99).

The sky is full of light:

lumine sic tremulo terra et cava caerula candent (R. 251).

---

[13] MSS. *quamquam; tam quam*, Baehrens.

[14] Also B. 416; R. 177; 374.

Epithets express chiefly magnitude: *altisonus* (B. 360); (R. 177); *caeruleus* (B. 416); *caerulus* (B. 28. 15; 54); (R. 251); *candens* (R. 302); *cavus* (R. 95; 251); *ingens* (B. 455); (R. 374); *magnus* (B. 48; 511.4), (R. 163); *profundus* (B. 377); *vastus* (B. 467).

The sky is often metaphorically represented, the metaphors being derived from other forms of nature, or, more commonly, from the works of man. We find: *liquidas pilatasque aetheris oras* (B. 458);[15] *caeli fretum* (B. 466); (R. 331); *cava caeruleo caelo cortina* (B. 416);[16] *pilam mediam coli* (B. 386); *caeli palatum* (B. 570); *cenacula maxima caeli* (B. 48); *altisono caeli clipeo* (R. 177); *caeli ingentes fornices* (R. 374); *ingens porta caeli* (B. 455); *caeli maxima porta* (B. 511.4).

It is identified with Jupiter:

aspice hoc sublimen candens, quem invocant omnes Iovem (R. 302).[17]

Juppiter hic risit, tempestatesque serenae[18]
riserunt omnes risu Iovis omnipotentis (B. 315).

It is appealed to, also, without the expression of such iden-tification:

O magna templa caelitum, commixta stellis splendidis! (R. 163).[19]

cupido cepit miseram nunc me proloqui
caelo atque terrae Medeai miserias (R. 216).[20]

occurring apparently in the same connection.

The sun is many times represented;[21] its eclipse is noted (B. 117); and its rising and setting (B. 55.14).

Sun   Epithets are: *albus* (B. 55.14); (*iubar*, B. 314); *aureus* (B. 55.17); *candens* (*fax*, R. 234); *candidus* (*lux*, B.

---

[15] luminis oras B. 73.5, 104.

[16] The text is very doubtful.

[17] Cf. B. 507.

[18] Cf. B. 354.

[19] Also B. 28.15.

Cf. ὦ στεροπὰ Διός, ὦ σκοτία νύξ.   (Eur. *Hec.* 68.)

[20] ὥσθ' ἵμερός μ'ὑπῆλθε γῇ τε κοιράνῳ
λέξαι μολούσῃ δεῦρο Μηδείας τύχας.   Eur. *Med.* 57.

[21] Mueller adds:
cum soles tandem faciunt langiscere longei (*A nn.* 493).

55.15); (*rota*, B. 335); *obstipus* (*lumen*, B. 202); *summus* (R. 237).

Personification is the commonest method of representing the sun:

> interea facit albus iubar Hyperionis cursum (B. 314).
>
> Sol, qui candentem in caelo sublimat facem (R. 234);
>
> Sol equis iter repressit ungulis volantibus (B. 4C7.3);
>
> Iuppiter tuque adeo summe Sol, qui res omnis spicis,
> quique tuo (cum) lumine mare terram caelum contines,
> inspice hoc facinus, prius quam fiat: prohibesseis scelus (R. 237).[22]

Moon

Apart from the sun's eclipse in which she figures the moon is mentioned only once.[23]

> Sole Luna luce lucet alba leni lactea (B. 507a).[24]

Stars

Stars are usually represented as adornments of the sky and of night.

The most unique description is the following:

> Quid noctis videtur in altisono
> caeli clipeo?
> . . . . . . temo superat
> stellas cogens etiam atque etiam
> noctis sublime iter (R. 177).[25]

Stars are described by epithet as *ardens* (B. 237); *fulgens* (B. 47; 113); *ingens* (*signum*, B. 150); *splendidus* (R. 163).

Clouds

Clouds are described as the home of the storm, in one fragment of the *Achilles*:

> per ego deum sublimas subices
> *umidas*, unde oritur imber sonitu saevo et spiritu (R. 2).

---

[22] Cf. Eur., *Med.* 1251.

> ἰὼ Γᾶ τε καὶ παμφαὴς
> ἀκτὶς Ἀελίου. κατίδετ᾽ ἴδετε τὰν
> ὀλομέναν γυναῖκα.

[23] Unless R. 251, refers to it.

[24] Attributed to Ennius' first by Baehrens.

[25] Cf. Eur., *Iph In Aul.* 6.

> Αγ. τίς ποτ᾽ ἄρ᾽ ἀστὴρ ὅδε πορθμεύει;
> Ιlρ. Σείριος, ἐγγὺς τῆς ἑπταπόρου
> Πλειάδος ἄσσων ἔτι μεσσήρης.

Night represents obscurity:

Night
    ea libertas est . . . .
    aliae res obnoxiae nocte in obscura latent (R. 259).

The sun sinks into the abyss of night, *infera noctis* (B. 55.15), and silent night enfolds the dead:

    omnes occisi obcensique in nocte serena (B. 265).

Epithets are: *intempestus* (B. 18; 121); *obscurus* (R. 259); *serenus* (B. 265).

Night, like the sun, is almost always personified. She pursues her journey on high, *noctis sublime iter* (R. 180),

    hinc Nox processit stellis ardentibus apta (B. 237).

    Nox quando mediis signis praecincta volabit (B. 281).

    (nox) quae cava caeli
    signitenentibus conficis bigis [26] — (R. 95).

Night "with impartial hand" interrupts a battle:

    bellum aequis manibus nox intempesta diremit (B. 121).

The only interesting description of winds is borrowed quite literally from Homer. The simile illustrates a battle:

Wind

    concurrunt veluti venti, cum spiritus austri
    imbricitor aquiloque suo cum flamine contra
    indu mari magno fluctus extollere certant [27] (B. 304).

They are described as roughening the sea:

    et aequora salsa ingentibus ventis veges (B. 498).

and as roaring with flame:

    cum magno strepitu Volcanum ventus vegebat (B. 384).

[26] Cf. Eur. *Andromeda*, fr. 114. N.
    ὦ νὺξ ἱερά,
    ὡς μακρὸν ἵππευμα διώκεις
    ἀστεροειδέα νῶτα διφρεύουσ'
    αἰθέρος ἱρᾶς
    τοῦ σεμνοτάτου δι' Ὀλύμπου.
[27] Cf. *Il.* 9. 4.
    "ὡς δ' ἄνεμοι δύο πόντον ὀρίνετον ἰχθυόεντα,
    Βορέης καὶ Ζέφυρος, τώ τε Θρῄκηθεν ἄητον,
    ἐλθόντ' ἐξαπίνης. ἄμυδις δέ τε κῦμα κελαινὸν
    κορθύεται, πολλὸν δὲ παρὲξ ἅλα φῦκος ἔχευεν.

Epithets are: *crudelis* (*hiems*, B. 151); *furens* (B. 425); *imbricitor* (*spiritus Austri* (B. 304); *ingens* (B. 498); *saevos* (*turbo*, B. 383).

They are personalized by the use of *imbricitor*, *furens*, and in the following:

> . . . . . vestro sine momine, venti (B. 426).

One simile and one metaphor are taken from rain:

> undique conveniunt velut imber tela tribuno (B. 299);

Rain   hastati spargunt hastas, fit ferreus imber (B. 201).

The sound of the rain is noted:

> . . . . ager oppletus imbrium
> fremitu . . . . . (R. 343).

There is a bare statement of the succession of seasons, **Seasons** B. 296, designating winter as *acer*.

From the sea are borrowed words to describe mist:

> transnavit cita per teneras caliginis auras (B. 19);

Sea   the sky: *caeli fretum* (B. 466); (R. 331); *aetheris oras* (B. 458), *luminis oras* (B. 73.5; 104); the earth: *campi* . . . *caerula* (*laetaque prata*) (B. 346), (p. 106).

A horseman is *gubernator* (B. 246).

Other figures are:

> fluctus verborum aures aucupant (R. 218);
>
> semper adundantes hastas frangitque quatitque (B. 238.5);
>
> .   .   .   praeda exercitus undat (B. 215);

A rough sea is often represented. Its shore:

> mare saxifragis undis   .   .   (B. 463).

Its prey tossed about upon the waves:

> rursus prorsus reciprocat fluctus fera (R. 103):
>
> alia fluctus differt dissupat
> visceratim membra, maria salso spumant sanguine (R. 105).

Its surface reddened by a flash of lightning:

> .   .   .   .   interea fax
> occidit oceanumque rubra tractim obruit aethra (B. 232).

Boats of various sorts are often represented: [28]

> ratibusque fremebat
> imber Neptuni (B. 400);
>
> labitur uncta carina per aequora cana celocis (B. 349);
>
> carbasus alta volat pandam ductura carinam (B. 452);
>
> Ostia munita est; idem locus naribus pulcris
> munda facit nautisque mari quaesentibus vitam (B. 101);
>
> verrunt extemplo palmae mare marmore pulso:
> caeruleum spumat sale conferta rate flavom (B. 258). [29]

The sound of the sea is probably referred to in the words *litora lata sonunt* (B. 261). It is *imber Neptuni*, (B. 400), *fluctus natantes* (B. 402).

Many of the epithets applied to it express color. They are:

altus (R. 74; 265); (B. 254; 350; 401); *asper* (*unda*, B. 467); *caeruleus* (B. 258); *caerulus* (B. 103; 417; 419); *canus* (B. 349); *flavos* (B. 258); *magnus* (B. 304.3; 532); (R. 50); *saevos* (*Neptunus*, B. 467.2); *salsus* (B. 100; 418, *aequora*, B. 498); *undans* (*salum* R. 162); [30]

Transferred from the sky to the sea is the term *velivolus* (B. 260); (R. 74), representing the ship as a bird.

The sea is described with figures taken from other forms of nature, as *ponti caerula prata* (B. 103); and as *marmor* (B. 258).

It is invested with life:

> inde Parum, circum quam caerula salsa ululabant (B. 418);
>
> mulserat huc navem compulsam fluctibus pontus (B. 165) [31]

---

[28] B. 102; 166; 167; 163; 169; 254; 259; 334; 350; 352; 353; 401. R. 52; 74.

[29] Quoted and explained by Gellius (2. 26. 21), "non enim videbatur caeruleum mare cum marmore flavo convenire. Sed cum sit ita, ut dixisti, flavus color e viridi et albo mixtus, pulcherrime prorsus spumas virentis maris 'flavom marmor' appellavit," with the following text, which Mueller retains:

> verrunt extemplo placide mare marmore flavo
> caeruleum spumat mare conferta rate pulsum.

[30] Mueller gives also *rapax unda* (*Ann.* 27).

[31] Manuscript reading. Baehrens emends to:

> mulserat huc navis compulsa fluctibus ponti.

It is uncertain whether the words *ita magni fluctus eici-*
Streams   *ebantur* (R. 9), in the *Achilles*, are used literally
of the Scamander, or figuratively of war.
There are gushing springs (B. 406). The Tiber pouring
into the salt sea (B. 100), a sluggish stream:

> quod per amoenam urbem leni fluit agmine flumen (B. 124).

Epithets are: *candidus* (B. 322) in contrast to a river pol-
luted with blood; *magnus* (R. 9); *perennis* (B. 467.4); *sanctus*
(B. 34) of the Tiber; *sulpureus* (B.186) of the waters of the
Nar.

Father Tiber is called upon (B. 34) and the same sort of
mythological personification occurs in the following:

> atque manu magna Romanos inpulit amnis (B. 309);
>
> constitit, credo, Scamander (R. 151) (cf. B. 38);

Mountains are of little interest. The aspect already
shown by Livius and Naevius, is seen in the
Mountains   reference to *ardua tesca aspera saxa* (B. 342),
and even the mountain of the Muses is *Musarum scopulos*
(B. 155.3). In addition to this aspect is that of utility, in
affording a wide view;

> ibi tum derepente ex alto in altum despexit mare (R. 208),

and caverns, probably for places of concealment (B. 301).
There are also:

> montibus obstipis obstantibus, unde oritur nox (B. 280).

The *Ripaean Mountains* (B. 491) and *Pelion* (R. 205), are
mentioned.

Epithets are: *arduus* (R. 342); *asper* (R. 342); *obstipus*
(B. 280); *tescus* (R. 342); *summus* (*montibus summis Ripaeis*,
B. 421).

Woods are a source of timber (B. 140), and in connection
with swamps, places useful for purposes of
Woods   concealment:

> silvarum saltus, latebras lamasque lutosas (B. 388).

They are described as *alta arbusta* (B. 140), and *frondosa
silva* (B. 140.5).

Trees
Of individual trees, Ennius has more to say. In her dream Ilia moves *per amoena salicta et ripas* (B. 28.5), and there is interest in the description·tions of individual trees elsewhere: *fici dulciferae* (B. 41);

longique cupressi
stant rectis foliis et amaro corpore buxum (B. 185);
capitibus nutantis pinos rectosque cupressos (B. 374);

populea frus (B. 375), and many trees together:

incedunt arbusta per alta, securibus caedunt:
percellunt magnas quercus, exciditur ilex,
fraxinus frangitur atque abies consternitur alta,
pinus proceras pervortunt: omne sonabat
arbustum fremitu silvai frondosai (B. 140).

Epithets applied to individual trees usually express height: *altus (abies,* B. 140.3); *amoenus (salicta,* B. 28.5); *longus (cupressus,* B. 140.2); *magnus (quercus,* B. 140.2); *procerus (pinus,* B. 140.4); *rectus (cupressus,* B. 374).

In the expression *omne sonabat arbustum fremitu silvai frondosai* (B. 140), the trees are regarded as suffering from the treatment received at the hands of the wood-cutters.

Aside from trees, plants are of little interest. The term *flos delibatus populi* (B. 222.6), is applied to M. Cethegus. From the ripening of fruits comes the expression *pugna praecoca* (B. 192).

The acanthus is mentioned B. 242. Varro. R. R. I. 48.2, says of Ennius, "*arista et granum omnibus fere notum, gluma paucis. itaque id apud Ennium solum scriptum scio esse, in Euhemeri libris versis* (B. 528). One fragment speaks of the separation of wheat from tares (B. 530),[32] and the familiar proverb to "look for a knot in a bulrush" is found B. 347.

The earth is partially personalized:

terraque corpus
quae dedit, ipsa capit neque dispendi facit hilum (B. 9).

Fields that produce crops are *laetus (ager,* B. 382); *(terrae frugiferae* (B. 428). Other fields are *laetus* (B. 346.3).

---

[32] Other references to agriculture are B. 206; 218; 405.

2

Animals are conspicuous in Ennius. They are, however,
almost confined to the *Annals* and *Satires.*

Animals   Birds are *praepes genus altivolantum* (B. 55.6);
pulcherrima .... *praepes avis* (B. 55.16); *genus pinnis
condecoratum* (B. 6). Those mentioned by name are the
peacock (B. 10). cock (R. 356), swan (B. 12), vulture (B. 93),
and eagle. The last is described picturesquely in the
words:

> et densis aquila pinnis obnixa volabat
> vento (B. 107).

snake with the epithet *caeruleus* (in the furies' hair) is mentioned in R. 28.

The monkey, *turpissima bestia,* is noticed for its resem-
blance to human beings (B. 490). The Roman wolf appears
in the *Annals* (B. 39; 40; 42). The elephant B. 137; 171.

The horse is more often and more fully represented than
any other animal. Ennius compares his own old age to
that of a race horse:

> hic, ut *fortis* equos, spatio qui saepe supremo
> vicit Olimpia, nunc senio confectus quiescit (B. 273).

Another figure is imitated closely from Homer:

> et tum sicut equos, qui de praesepibus fartus
> vincla suis magnis animis abrumpit et inde
> fert sese campi per caerula laetaque prata
> celso pectore, saepe iubam quassat simul altam,
> spiritus ex anima calida spumas agit albas (B. 346).[33]

The strength and high spirit of the horse is again described:

> ducit quadrupedum biiugam (vim), invitam domat,
> ovalida quorum infrenast nimis tenacia (R. 156).

-----

[33] ὡς δ' ὅτε τις στατὸς ἵππος, ἀκοστήσας ἐπὶ φάτνῃ,
δεσμὸν ἀπορρήξας θείῃ πεδίοιο κροαίνων,
εἰωθὼς λούεσθαι ἐυρρεῖος ποταμοῖο,
κυδιόων· ὑψοῦ δὲ κάρη ἔχει, ἀμφὶ δὲ χαῖται
ὤμοις ἀίσσονται· ὁ δ' ἀγλαΐηφι πεποιθώς,
ῥίμφα ἑ γοῦνα φέρει μετά τ' ἤθεα καὶ νομὸν ἵππων. *Il.* 6, 506.

sublimiter

quadrupedantes . . . flammam halitantes (R. 153);

cumque gubernator magna contorsit equom vi (B. 317).

denique vi magna quadrupes eques atque elephanti
proiciunt sese (B. 171);[34]

and the sound of horses hoofs, *summo sonitu quatit ungula
terram* (B. 196); (also B. 300).

The young dog which barks before its teeth are grown
is used in a simile (B. 410), the verb *latrare* in *animus cum
pectore latrat* (B. 441); *ululare* of the sea (B. 418).[35]

The hunting dog is several times described:

siquando veluti vinclis venatica *velox*
apta dolet, si forte feras ea nare sagaci
sensit, voce sua et nictit ululatque ibi acuta (B. 235);

invictus canis atque *sagax* et naribus fretus (B. 385);

Other domestic animals are cattle (B. 135); (R. 255); from
which too the term *mugire* comes, used figuratively in
tibicina maximo labore mugit;[36] sheep:

propter stagnas, ubi lanigerum pecus piscibus pascit (B. 492);

pigs, *sues stolidi* (B. 61).

The sky, the sea, trees, animals are especially interesting in Ennius, and most of all the sky. In
Summary   other poets the clouds and heavenly bodies
find better representation, but in none is the sky itself described in such varied terms. Its form is most often represented, yet its color and brilliance are also conspicuous.

Indeed, epithets denoting these qualities are freely used
not only of the sky and heavenly bodies, but of the sea and
of streams as well.

---

[34] See Gell. XVIII.5.

[35] Varro, *L. L.* VII. 104, derives this metaphor from the howling of the
wolf. Other references to dogs B. 473: R. 404.

[36] The verb *boare*, in *clamore bovantes* (B. 442), is explained by Varro
L. L. VII. 103 (see also Non. 79.4), as transferred from cattle to men.
Whether the poet who used the expression agreed with Varro in consider-
ing it a figure, cannot be determined.

Of artistic beauty and picturesqueness in nature, apart
from what is expressed by epithets, little is shown. What
there is, is found in some of the descriptions of trees, the
sky and heavenly bodies. The account of the auspices
taken by Romulus and Remus is enhanced by the natural
setting given it: [37]

> interea sola currus recessit in infera Noctis
> exin candida se radiis dedit acta foras lux,
> et simul ex alto longe pulcherruma praepes
> multa volavit avis; simul aureus exoritur sol,
> cedunt de caelo ter quattuor corpora sancta
> avium, praepetibus sese pulchrisque locis dant (B. 55.14).

In a passage in the satires, various forms of nature are
grouped as in a picture:

> mundus caeli vastus constitit silentio,
> et Neptunus saevos undis asperis pausam dedit;
> Sol equis iter repressit ungulis volantibus,
> constitere amnes perennes, arbores vento vacant (B. 467).

Most characteristic of Ennius' treatment of nature is its
strongly imaginative character. There are many figures
representing one form of nature in terms borrowed from
another, as "blue meadows of sea;" or from man's works,
as "shield of the sky;" and less frequently human affairs
in terms of nature, as "waves of words," "a hail of
spears."

Nature is in many cases invested with life, and sometimes definitely personified. In some of these cases, nota-
bly in the very Greek descriptions of the sun and night, is
found the nearest approach to the modern sympathetic or
sentimental view of nature, though they lean rather to the
true mythological representation. Particularly in the representations of the sun and night, but also in other passages, Ennius has been shown to depend largely on Greek
originals. [38] Yet, in many cases, differences will be found

---

[37] Biese, p. 10.

[38] Die wirkungsvollste Effekte sind den Griechischen Tragikern entlehnt,
wenn wir auch nicht alle Einzelheiten belegen können. Biese, p. 12.

great enough to give his lines an independent character of their own. These differences generally lie in the larger descriptive element in the Latin. The Greek "O light of day, O dark night" (Eur. *Hec.* 68), becomes "O ye great realm of the gods, strewn with glittering stars " (R. 165). Eur. *Med.* 1253, "O earth and all-seeing light of the sun," becomes "O Jupiter and thou too supreme sun, who dost see all things and dost enfold seas, land and sky with thy light " (R. 237). The simile from the conflict of the winds (B. 304) is borrowed closely from Homer (*Il.* 9. 4) yet adds the descriptive epithet *imbricitor*, and the name of the south wind, while the famous simile from the horse (B. 346) adds several touches to its Homeric prototype (*Il.* 6. 506), as "the blue-green fields and glad pastures." Most clearly borrowed from the Greek are the complaint to the heavens of the woes of Medea (R. 216; Eur. *Med.* 57); the description of night in her starry chariot (R. 95; Eur. *Andromeda* fr. 114). It is likewise true that an Euripidean tone is evident in other fragments whose definite Greek source cannot be named. Even in the *Annals*,[39] many references to the sky and night occur which are strikingly Euripidean in character, and lead to the inference that the phraseology of the Greek dramatists, become familiar through much study and translation of his works, remained in the mind of the Latin writer and came to the surface even when in his later years he was writing epic poetry of a purely Roman character. The peculiar and grotesque description of the sky, however, seems to be purely Roman, or rather, perhaps, "Ennian."

4.   PACUVIUS.[40]

The fragments of Pacuvius' tragedies are about three hundred in number. The proportion containing r ferences to nature is smaller than in Ennius, being only a out one-

---

[39] See personification of night, B. 237; 281; of the sun, B. 314; 335.

[40] References are to Ribbeck.

eighth. The subject matter and character of these fragments, too, is noticeably different.

The sky is as meagerly represented in Pacuvius as it is
Sky   fully in Ennius. The only interesting description of it occurs in the Chryses, and is philosophic rather than aesthetic in character:

> hoc vide, circum supraque quod complexu continet terram
> solisque exortu capessit candorem, occasu nigret,
> id quod nostri caelum memorant, Grai perhibent aethera:
> quidquid est hoc, omnia animat format alit auget creat
> sepelit recipitque in sese omnia, omniumque idem est pater,
> indidemque eadem aeque oriuntur de integro atque eodem occidunt,
> (Pac. 86.)

The idea is carried on in the following:

> mater terrast: parit haec corpus, animam [autem] aeter adiugat (93).[41]

In the *Antiopa* the words

> sol si perpetuo siet,
> *flammeo* vapore torrens terrae fetum exusserit:
> nocti ni interveniat, fructus per pruinam obriguerint (12),

are probably used in a simile illustrating the value of al-
ternating good and bad fortunes for men.

The rising of the sun is referred to 87; 347; its setting
87; 411. Elsewhere, both sun and night are personified:

> te, Sol, invoco, ut mihi potestatem duis
> inquirendi mei parentis (219).

> exorto iubare, noctis decurso itinere (347).

Dawn is pictured:

> . . . terra exhalat auram ad auroram *umidam* (363).

One metaphor is taken from the mist:

> Quid istuc est? vultum caligat quae tristitas? (53).

---

[41] This resembles closely a fragment of Euripides' *Chrysippus:* Fr. 839
(Nauck).

> Χωρεῖ δ'ὀπίσω
> τὰ μὲν ἐκ γαίας φύντ' εἰς γαῖαν
> τὰ δ' ἀπ' αἰθερίου βλαστόντα γονῆς
> εἰς οὐράνιον πάλιν ἦλθε πόλον.

The only other reference to phenomena of the atmos-
phere is a figure from snow and hail:

> nivit sagittis, plumbo et saxis grandinat (*Praetext.* 4).

The wind, *saevi turbines*, is an element in the description
Wind   of a storm at sea (415), and is again mentioned
in 76.

The sea is often described.   There is the shore: *ut stag-
norum umorem rimarem* (203); the tide: *aesti forte
Sea   ex arido* (97);[12] the sound of the sea, *murmur
maris* (417).[13]   It is designated as *altum* (332).   The change
from storm to calm is described in the Chryses:

> interea loci
> flucti flacciscunt, silescunt venti, mollitur mare (76).

The rising of a storm from calm, more fully:

> profectione laeti piscium lasciviam
> intuentur, nec tuendi satietas capier potest.
> interea prope iam occidente sole inhorrescit mare,
> tenebrae conduplicantur, noctisque et nimbum obcaecat nigror,
> flamma inter nubes coruscat, caelum tonitru contremit,
> grando mixta imbri largifico subita praecipitans cadit,
> undique omnes venti erumpunt, saevi existunt turbines,
> fervit aestu pelagus (409).

The disaster of the ship is shown:

> rapide retro citroque percito aestu praecipitem ratem
> reciprocare, undaeque e gremiis subiectare adtligere (333).

And in another fragment the confusion among ships in a
storm is pictured:

> armamentum stridor, flictus navium,
> strepitus fremitus, clamor tonitruum et rudentum sibilus (335.)

The personalization *undaeque e gremiis subiectare* (333) is
the only figurative representation of the sea.

---

[41] *Fluth nach der Ebbe* — Ribbeck, *Röm. Trag.* p. 251.
[43] Serv. in *Aen.* 1.55 — *quia ventos murmur sequitur.*

Mountains are somewhat more conspicuous in Pacuvius than in his predecessors. A high rock is

Mountains described:

climbed for the sake of a wide view, in the *Chryses* (95). In the same play a cave is described:

> est ibi sub eo saxo penitus strata harena ingens specus (99).

Rocks and steep places are the scenes where tragic events occur in the *Periboea:*

> ardua per loca agrestia pes
> trepidante gradu nititur (272).

in the *Dulorestes* (136), and in one fragment of uncertain location (350). The wild rocky regions of the Bacchae are shown in the *Periboea* (310); uncultivated valleys in the *Atalanta:*

> cum incultos pervestigans rimarem sinus (71).

Inculta vastitudine (314), *desertitudines* (438), and

> qua vix caprigeno generi gradilis gressio est (*Practext.* 5),

may well refer to mountain regions. Aetna is mentioned (252), and Ida:

> Idae promunturium, quoius lingua in altum proicit (94).

All epithets denote very much the same characteristics. There are *ardua loca* (272); *loca horrida* (1.b); *scrupea saxa* (310); *aspera saxa* (351); *scruposam specum* (252).

Hills are personalized in

> clamore et sonitu colles resonantes bount[44] (223).

The metaphor *flos Liberi* occurs (291). Consistently with

Plants

the philosophic ideas in the *Chryses*, the earth is personalized (363). In the *Dulorestes* she refuses her fruits in consequence of Aegisthus' crime:

> nec grandiri frugum fetum posse nec mitiscere (142).

---

[44] See page 107.

Animals   The halcyon appears in a comparison:

alcyonis ritu litus pervolgans feror (393).

Snakes or dragons are described:

linguae bisulcis actu crispo fulgere (229);

and again 398; the turtle (2); the dolphin;

Nerei *repandirostrum incurvicervicum* pecus (408);

wild beasts, *ferae* and *beluae* (303; 357).

Fear of death in animals is described:

quin etiam ferae
quibus abest ad praecavendum intellegendi astutia
mortis iniecto terrore horrescunt (357).

Herds of cattle are *cornifrontes armentas*[45] (349); goats, *caprigeno generi* (*Praetext*. 5); the dog is found:

nam canis, quando est percussa lapide, non tam illum adpetit,
qui sese icit, quam illum eumpse lapidem, qui ipsa icta est, petit (38).

The sea is described with force and vividness.[46] The rela-
Summary   tion of earth and sky is interestingly set forth in the *Chryses*. Otherwise Pacuvius' treatment of nature is not of great interest. It is noticeable that epithets are very few, and include no color terms.

5.   ACCIUS.[47]

Of Accius' poetry about four hundred and sixty fragments remain. The proportion referring to nature is the same as in the case of Ennius' tragedies, one-sixth.

The sky is described as resounding with thunder (Acc.
Sky   223), echoing with the shouts of men (*Prae-text*. 2), changing from bright to dark:

splendet saepe, ast idem nimbis interdum nigret (200).

---

[44] 121 also refers to cattle.

[46] Of these only, is Biese's statement true:

"Immerhin zeigt Pacuvius bereits hohe Empfänglichkeit für poetische Naturschilderungen die er mit Ferve und Pracht entwirft" (p. 16); and even of these it can hardly be said "In den Naturschilderungen verrät sich der Maler, besonders die Seestücken" (p. 15), unless the painter may be regarded as putting in the strokes before our eyes. Both calm and storm are shown as gradually coming on, not as fully developed in a picture.

[47] References are to Ribbeck unless otherwise specified.

Some expressions closely resemble Ennius:
aequora caeli (224); *templum caelitum (Praetext.* 2); *alto
ab limine caeli* (531).

Lux stands for day (37).

The sun is *orbem flammeum radiatum (Praetext.* 27); *radia-*
Sun   *tum lumen* (584); its rays are, *ardens* (493).

It is personified:

> Sol qui *micantem candido* curru atque equis
> flammam citatis *fervido* ardore explicas,
> quianam tam adverso augurio et inimico omine
> Thebis *radiatum* lumen ostentas tuum? (581)."

Moon   Time is measured by the moon's course in 100.

Orion is the type of changelessness:" *citius Orion pallescit*
(693). The signs of the zodiac are described:

Stars   pervade polum, *splendida* mundi
sidera binis continuis sex
picti spoliis (678).

The Argo is compared to a cloud by the shepherd who
has never seen a ship: *interruptum credas nim-*
Clouds   *bum volvier* (395).

The darkening of the sky by clouds is expressed by the
verb *nigrere* (260).

Decriptions of dawn are relatively numerous:

Dawn   iamque auroram rutilare procul
cerno (675).

It is in the early morning light that Astyanax is captured
and taken to Ulysses:

> hic per matutinum lumen tardo procedens gradu
> derepente aspicio ex nemore pavidum et properantem egredi (183).

" Eur. *Phoen. Prolog.* 1:

"ὦ τὴν ἐν ἄστροις οὐρανοῦ τέμνων ὁδὸν
καὶ χρυσοκολλήτοισιν ἐμβεβὼς δίφροις
Ἥλιε, θοαῖς ἵπποισιν εἰλίσσων φλόγα,
ὡς δυστυχῆ Θήβαισι τῇ τόθ' ἡμέρᾳ
ἀκτῖν' ἐφῆκας.

⁴⁰According to Ribbeck: " Er könnte auch zu Anfang des Stückes die
Unbeugsamkeit seines Sinnes betheuren." *Röm. Trag.*, p. 545.

The earth at dawn is described in 493. (p. 119.)

Night   Night is a time of misfortune:

> deum regnator nocte caeca caelum e conspectu abstulit (32).
>
> nocte intempesta nostram devenit domum (*Praetext.* 41).

The most interesting description of wind occurs in the
Wind   *Philoctetes*, probably in a comparison:

> sub axe posita ad stellas septem, unde horrifer
> Aquiloni' stridor gelidas molitur nives (500).

The winter wind is described in the *Prometheus:*

> tum profusus flamine hiberno gelus (290);

and the breeze that carries the ship:

> .   .   .   vela ventorum animae immittere (10),

in the *Myrmidones.*

Snow   The only reference to snow or rain is:

> cum ninxerint caelestium molem mihi (101).[50]

The figure *belli fluctus* is found in 608.

     The salt waves of the sea are sought by
Sea   Philoctetes in the pain of his wound (562).
     The effect of a neighboring mountain in calm-
ing the waves is noted (629, *Telephus*). The sea appears
as the home of the exile:

> nunc per terras vagus, extorris,
> regno exturbatus, mari (333).

In the *Medea* the Argo is built:

> ut tristis turbinum
> toleraret hiemes, mare cum horreret fluctibus (412).

The sound of the waves on the shore and the echoes among
the rocks is described:

---

[50] Soll man *nubes*, oder wenn die Variant *ninxerit* vorzuziehen wäre,
Juppiter als subject suppliren, und an Schneemassen denken, die sich zu
den von Neptun gesandten Fluthen gesellt haben, um das Land des Königs
zu überschwemmen? Ribbeck, *Röm. Trag.*, p. 562.

hac ubi curvo litore latratu
unda sub undis labunda sonit (569);

simul et circum magna sonantibus
excita saxis suavisona[51] echo
crepitu clangente cachinnat (571).[52]

Ships are often mentioned,[53] but by far the most interesting description is that given by the shepherd who had
never seen a ship before:

tanta moles labitur
fremibunda ex alto ingenti sonitu et spiritu.
prae se undas volvit. vertices vi suscitat:
ruit prolapsa, pelagus respargit reflat.
ita dum interruptum credas nimbum volvier,
dum quod sublime ventis expulsum rapi
saxum aut procellis, vel globosos turbines
existere ictos undis concursantibus:
nisi quas terrestris pontus strages conciet,
aut forte Triton fuscina evertens specus
supter radices penitus undante in freto
molem ex profundo saxeam ad caelum erigit (391).

Epithets used of the sea are varied: *altus* (*stagna*, 335);
inmisericors (*fluctus* 33); *salsus* (*fluctus*, 563); *undans* (*fretus*,
401).

The shore is *anfractus* (336); *curvus* (569).

The sea is invested with life in the expression *latratu sonit*
(569), and in

flucti inmisericordes iacere, taetra ad saxa adlidere (33).

Streams   Envy is compared to a stream that eats away
the rock:

saxum id facit angustitatem. et sub eo saxo exuberans
scatebra fluviae radit rupem (504).

---

[51] *sacra sonando*, MSS.

[52] Quite different is the effect of the echo in Philoctetes' cave, where it
adds to the dreariness:

in tecto umido
quod eiulatu questu gemitu fremitibus
resonando mutum flebilis voces refert (549).

[53] 10; 14; 125; 123; 405; 482; 522; 574; 575; 629; 677 (shipwrecked sailors)..

Flucti cruoris . . . *Mysii* is found 633. By name are mentioned the Scamander:

> Scamandriam undam salso sanctam obtexi sanguine
> atque acervos alta in amni corpore explevi hostico
> (322 *Epinausimache*);

the Inachus, *rapidas undas Inachi* (297, *Epigoni*); Dirce, (602, *Thebais*),[54] Alpheus (509).

Epithets are: *abundans* (297); *altus* (323); *rapidus (unda*, 297); *sanctus (Scamander*, 322).

The usual aspect of desolation and dreariness is presented.

Mountains In the *Andromeda* are:

> misera obvalla saxo sento, paedore alguque et fame (111).

In the *Philoctetes*,

> . . . . deserta et tesqua. . . . . loca (554),[55]

and the cavern which reechoes with his lament (549).[56] Other aspects of mountains are shown. There are pasture grounds for flocks:

> in celsis montibus
> pecua atque inter colles pascunt Danai in Froegiae terminis
> (177), (cf. 409).

The picturesque expression,

> colomen alte geminis aptum cornibus (650),

probably refers to Parnassus.

In the *Bacchae:*

> sanctus Cithaeron
> frondet viridantibus fetis (243),

and the Bacchic chorus is shown:

> laetum iu Parnaso inter pinos tripudiantem in circulis (249),

Mount Oetaeon is the scene of Hercules' death in 670.

---

[54] One more reference is found in 461.

[55] Cf. description in Sophocles, *Phil.* 220.

> ἰὼ ξένοι
> τίνες ποτ᾽ εἰς γῆν τήνδε ναυτίλῳ πλάτῃ
> κατέσχετ᾽ οὔτ᾽ εὔορμον οὔτ᾽ οἰκουμένην.

[56] For similar scenes, see 81; 557.

Mountain regions are described as: *celsus* (177); *sentus* (*saxum*, 111); *miser* (*obvallum*, 111); *tesquus* (*locus desertus*, 554); *sanctus* (*Cithaeron*, 243).

In addition to the references to woods in con-
Woods nection with mountains, are found *silvicolae*
(237) and

vagent ruspantes silvas, sectantes feras (441, *Meleager*).[57]

Plants   *Flos* is used figuratively:

num quis non mortalis florem liberum invidit meum ? (424)

and the verb *florere* in the expression *insignibus florere* (632, *Telephus*).

Of individual trees the pine (249), the ash

fraxinus fusa ferox infensa infinditur ossis (B. Acc. 4)

and the fir (331; 407) alone are mentioned.

A comparison is made between the good and wicked of mankind and good and poor grain:[58]

probae etsi in segetem sunt deteriorem datae
fruges, tamen ipsae suapte natura enitent (234, *Thyestes*).

A rich harvest field is again figuratively used in the *Andromeda* (115). The plain of Amphissa beneath Parnassus (probably) is described as:

Locrorum late viridia et frugum ubera (49, *Erigona*),

and the effect of the gods' displeasure upon the harvest is shown:

. . . fruges prohibet pergrandescere (440, *Meleager*).

The vine leaf *glauco pampino* (257, *Bacchae*), and the verbena (472, *Neoptolemus*) are used as decorations and in religious observances.

---

[57] For another reference to mountain regions and woods see R. 435.

[58] "Ein gemeiner Saatfeld könne durch Pflege edele Frucht hervorbringen, ebensoleicht aber pflege eine edele Mutter von einem niedergesinnten Manne des Stammes unwürdige Nachkommen zu gebaren." Ribb. *Röm. Trag.* p. 451.

Cf. Eurip. *Hec.* 592.

The farmer's labor at early dawn is described:

> forte ante auroram, radiorum ardentum indicem,
> cum e somno in segetem agrestis cornutos cient,
> ut rorulentas terras ferro fumidas
> proscindant glebasque arvo ex mollito excitent (493, *Ocnomaus*).

Animals

Pinniger is used of birds (546, *Philoctetes*).
The eagle is mentioned B. 8.

The dolphin is used in a figure:

> sicut lasciui atque alacres rostris perfremunt
> delphini (403, *Medea*).

There are found also the serpent:

> eius serpentis squamae squalido auro et purpura pertextae
>   (517, *Pelopidae*);

the boar:

> frigit saetas rubore ex oculis fulgens flammeo (443),

in the *Meleager*.   Skins of wild animals deck the Bacchae:

> tunc silvestrum exuvias laevo pictas lateri accommodant (256).[59]

Of domestic animals are found the sheep, *pecus lanigerum*
(*Praetext.* 19); the goat, *caprigenum trita ungulis* (544); the
pig (B. 22); herds deserted by their shepherds:

> vagant, pavore pecuda in tumulis deserunt.
> (a) qui vos pascet postea (409 *Medea*)

oxen, *agrestis cornutos* (494).[60]

Horses play the most important part among animals.
There is a simile:

> item ac maestitiam mutam infantum quadrupedum (315)[61]

Freno is figuratively used, *iram infrenes* (15), *effrenata
inpudentia* (133).   There are also *vim citatum quadrupedum*
(381),

> perite in stabulo frenos immitens *feris* (416);

and *quadripedantum sonipedum* (603).

---

[59] Cf. Eur. *Bacch.* 696.
[60] Other references to herds are 211; 271.
[61] Cf. *Il.* 17.426 ff.

References to dawn are especially noteworthy in Accius.

Summary   He excels in power of description of quiet scenes, of which the account of the ploughman's labor in the early morning is most interesting (p. 119). The same power of description is seen in the shepherd's story of the Argo, where there is also a touch of imagination not seen in any other passage (p. 116).

In the account of the capture of Astyanax in the dim light of early morning seems to be an attempt to suit the natural setting to the story. The same is seen in the description of Philoctetes' place of exile. And the expression "pitiless waves" (p. 116) shows at least in a negative way a sense of possible kinship between nature and man.

6. FRAGMENTS OF TRAGEDY OF DOUBTFUL AUTHORSHIP.[62]

Of these Ribbeck gives one hundred and fifty-five.

The sky is represented as *aeterna templa caeli* (Incert. 227).
Sky   It is invoked:

> teculit senilis Poeas ad caelum manus. (70);

The sun is personified:

> ore beato lumine volitans, qui per caelum candidus equitas! (183);

the dawn:

> sed iam se caelo cedens Aurora obstinet suum patrem (215); [63]

ght:

> Erebo (pro) creata *fuscis* crinibus Nox, te invoco (132).

Winds are addressed:

> agite o pelagi cursores
> cupidam in patriam portate! (253)

Sea   Misfortune is typified by shipwreck:

> naufragia, labes generis ignores, senex? (84);

> neque me patiar
> iterum ad unum scopulum ut olim
> classem Achivom offendere (139).

Ships are *rates repentes* (225),[64]

---

[62] References are to Ribbeck.

[63] Baehrens assigns to the *Carmen Nelei*.

[64] Other references to boats are 90; 181.

The shore is represented:

> qua ponto ab Helles atque ab Ionio mari
> urgetur Isthmus (105); [65]

its solitude:

> et ego ibo ut latebras ruspans rimer maritimas (83);
> litus atque aer, et solitudo mera (152).

The sea is *altus* (*aequor*, 224); *salum* (4).

The only mention of streams is in connection with Tan-
Streams and Mountains   talus (111).

A hillock is described:

> saxea est verruca in summo montis vertice (141);

the entrance to Acheron (73).

Plants A comparison between leafy branches and hair
is made:

> infulatas hostias
> non lana, sed velatas frondenti coma (220). [66]

The fields of Asia are *frugifera et ecferta* (164), *florens* is
metaphorically used, *florentissimo regno* (136); *omnia florere*
(136), vines are *vites laetificae* (134).

There is also a picture of the exuberance of all nature:

> caelum nitescere, arbores frondescere,
> vites laetificae pampinis pubescere,
> rami bacarum ubertate incurvescere,
> segetes largiri fruges, florere omnia,
> fontes scatere, herbis prata convestirier (131). [67]

Animals From the management of horses comes the
figure:

> erras erras: nam exultantem te et praefidentem tibi
> repriment validae legum habenae atque imperi insistent iugo (125).

---

[65] Other references to the Hellespont are 107; 163.
[66] MSS. *frondentis comas*.
[67] Probably from Ennius' *Eumenides;* cf. Aesch. *Eum.* 903:

> καὶ ταῦτα γῆθεν ἔκ τε ποντίας δρόσου
> ἐξ οὐρανοῦ τε κἀνέμων ἀήματα,
> εὐηλίως πνέοντ' ἐπιστείχειν χθόνα ·
> καρπόν τε γαίας καὶ βοτῶν ἐπίρρυτον
> ἀστοῖσιν εὐθενοῦντα μὴ κάμνειν χρόνῳ.

3

The speed of horses is vividly represented in the following:

> *agilis sonipes* rapitur celeri sonitu trepidans (237);
>
> rapite agite ruite *celeripedes!* (218);
>
> rapiunt per undas currus suspensos equi (196).

Of other animals are represented: *hostiis balantibus* (9); the bulls tamed by Jason (94).

7. HOSTIUS.

Animals

Of the seven fragments of Hostius, two are concerned with animals. Birds he calls *gentis altivolantum aetherias* (B. Host. 1). The fate of cattle in time of war is referred to:

> saepe greges pecuum ex hibernis pastibus pulsae (B. 4).

8. LUCILIUS.[68]

Of the nine hundred and forty-three fragments of Lucilius' satires, only about one-fourteenth have any reference to nature.

Sky

There is a reference to investigating nature:

> aetheris et terrae genitabile quaerere tempus (1);

a reference to moisture exhaled from the earth in the words:

> terra abit in nimbos imbremque (97).

Winds

Fair wind is mentioned:

> nec ventorum flamina flando suda secundet (673);
>
> rex Cotus ille duo hos uentos, austrum atque aquilonem,
> novisse aiebat me solos demagis, istos
> ex nimbo austellos nec nosse nec esse putare (381);

but more often stormy winds at sea:[69]

> continuo, simul ac paulo vehementius aura
> inflarit, fluctus erexerit extuleritque (757);
>
> nam si tu fluctus undasque e gurgite salso
> tollere decreris, venti prius Emathii vim,
> ventum, inquam. tollas (37).

---

[68] References are all to Baehrens' *Fragmenta Poetarum Romanorum*.
[69] Cf. also 291; 474.

Epithets are: *saevus* (*tempestas*, 430); *sudus* (*flamen*, 673).

Sea

Several of Lucilius' references to the sea are interesting. They all refer to navigation. Probably figurative is:

quodque te in tranquillum ex saevis transfert tempestatibus (430).

The cyclops staff is compared to a ship's mast (353.3). Dangers of navigation appear:[59]

vir mare metitur magnum et se fluctibus tradit (756);

saxa ad stridor ubique, rudentum sibilus instat (805).

The sea is called *sale* (231).

Epithets of the sea are only the most obvious: *magnus* (756); *salsus* (37).

Streams and Mountains

The "fountains of the muses" (699), the river Silarus (92), and even more insignificant references make up the list.

Mountains are only twice mentioned:

tanti se Emporiis montes εἰϛ aetera tollent (599)

αἰγίλιποι montes, Aetnae ocres, *asperi* Athones (79.4).

Plants   *Flos* is metaphorically used (787).

Thorns no doubt stand for trouble in *stat sentibus pectus* (148) which finds its literal prototype in *stat sentibus fundus* (870). There is the proverbial "knot in the bulrush" in 16.

Otherwise plants are shown only as articles of food, or in connection with agriculture, to which there are many references.[71] The only one of any interest is:

purpureamque uvam facit *albam* pampinam habere (727).

Animals   Many kinds of animals are shown.

The only wild birds, aside from those mentioned merely as articles of food, are the vulture (39), the diver, figuratively, *aerarius mergus*, 879.

---

[70]Other references to the sea and ships are: 90; 91; 92; 93; 231; 290; 888.

[71] 219; 379; 383; 398; 524.

From fowls, one simile is taken:

> candidus una
> ac bene plumalis quasi olorum atque auseris collus (218);

and one metaphor:

> usque petit pipans: 'da qualibet, ut iuvat' inquit (831).

The cock is described in 238.

In figures are found the lion, (207), the rhinoceros, the wolf in a metaphor, *vetulum lupum Annibalem* (654), the dolphin (211). Outside of figures are found the young of wild beasts (138), the lion (778; 780; 782), the elephant and camel (851), the monkey (850), the snake, (*colubra*, 408; *anguis volucris ac pinnatos* 462), the dolphin:

> lascivire pecus nasi rostrique repandum (174),

the whale and tunny fish (847), *timia* (765), *vermiculi* (216), scorpion, *scorpios cauda sublata* (708). Domestic animals generally appear in figures and illustrations, for comic effect:

> nequam et magnus homo, laniorum inmanis canes ut (184);
>
> . . . . . eodem pacto obgaunis (224).[72]

Once the comparison is reversed:

> inritata canes quam homo quam planius dicit (10).

Words belonging to the sounds made by animals, are often used of men:

> haec, inquam, rudet e rostris (189);
>
> quantum hinnitum atque eiulitatum (856).[73]

Pigs are found (282; 790); the horse in the following:

> sustineat currum ut bonus saepe agitator equosque (813).

Horses are spoken of in various terms: *gradarius, optumus vector* (349) ; *Campanus sonipes succussor* (368) ; *succussatoris, taetri tardique caballi* (78). The goat is described:

> pascali pecore ac montano, hirto atque soluce (788).

the sheep, *musimo* in 196, the ass 780; 895.

---

[72] The dog is also mentioned in 138; 773; 778.
[73] Other references to cattle are 187; 286; 697; 730; 752.

The treatment of animals in comic figures is interesting,
Summary otherwise Lucilius' treatment of nature is entirely uninteresting. Of sentiment for nature
no trace appears.

9. TITUS QUINTIUS ATTA.

One of the two fragments of Atta's epigrams contains a
figure from agriculture:

vertamus vomerem
in ceram mucroneique aremus osseo (T. Quint. Atta 2).

10. VALERIUS AEDITUUS.

A figure in one of the two epigrams shows a modern
touch:
Wind lucet pectoris flamma satis.
istam mox potis est vis *sacra* exstinguere venti
aut imber caelo concitus praecipitans (Val. Aed. 2.2).

11. QUINTUS LUTATIUS CATULUS.

Among the ten verses of his two fragments, is found
a comparison of the appearance of Aurora and
Dawn Roscius:

constiteram exorientem Auroram forte salutans,
quom subito a laeva Roscius exoritur.
pace mihi liceat, caelestes, dicere vestra;
mortalis visust pulcrior esse deo (Q. Lut. Cat. 2).

12. AULUS FURIUS ANTIAS.

Of the six fragments of Antias' epic verses, five contain
references to nature. In one is the odd expression:

omnia noctescunt tenebris caliginis *atrac* (A. Fur. Ant. 2).

Sea Two references to the sea are interesting:

sicut fulca levis volitat super aequora classis (4).

The changing color of the sea under the influence of the
wind is described:

spiritus Eurorum *viridis* cum purpurat undas (5).

Plants   A metaphor from the growth of plants is used:

increscunt animi, virescit volnere virtus (3).

13. PORCIUS LICINUS.

One of the four fragments is,

serena caeli momina et *salsi* fretus (Porc. Lic 6).

Tenerae propaginis (5), is used of lambs.

14. GNAEUS MATIUS.

In the translation of the Iliad, the one reference to nature, a river (Cn. Mat. 7) is unimportant. In
Sky   the *Mimiambi* is one pleasing picture of the
rising sun:

iamiam albicascit Phoebus et recentatur,
commune hominibus lumen et voluptatis (9).

Fragments 14; 16; 17 deal with agriculture. The adverb
columbulatim, is used of the expression of affection in 12.

15. SUEIUS.

Among the nine fragments of the idylls, is found the
Birds   figurative expression:

ascendit e frunde et fritinnit suaviter [74] (Sueius. 6).

16. LAEVIUS.

Of Laevius' poetry about thirty fragments remain. The
Sea   moon is *alma Noctiluca* (Laev. 26). The sea
and ships are referred to:

tu qui permensus ponti maria *alta* carina
relivola (11);

maria alta in 12; echo among rocks in 10.

17. CARMINA MARCIANA.

These prophetic verses contain references to the "great
sea," *pontum magnum* (*Carm. Marc.* 1.6), and the "fruitful
earth," *terra frugiferente* (1.6).

---

[74] Varro L. L. VII.104.

CHAPTER II.

CICERONIAN PERIOD.

1. CICERO.[75]

Cicero's prose writings would furnish some interesting material for this discussion, as Biese[76] has demonstrated. The poems alone, however, come within its scope. The greater part of what is left of Cicero's poetry is acknowledged translation from Aratus. These poems, dealing with astronomical and meteorological subjects as they do, furnish little of interest apart from their description of the heavenly bodies.

The sky is represented as *tegmine caeli* (281; 477; 483); *lumina caeli* (355; 653); *caeli* . . . *loca* (374); *caeli cavernas* (497); *aetheris cavernis* (B; M. T. Cicero 3.5); *convexum orbem* (560); *igniferum aethera* (329); *inmoderatum aethera* (B. 43). The sky with its stars is described:

Sky

> quattuor aeterno lustrantes lumine mundum
> orbes stelligeri portantes signa feruntur
> amplexi terras caeli sub tegmine fulti
> e quibus annorum volitantia lumina nosces,
> quae densis distincta licebit cernere signis (481).

In a translation of Euripides[77] it is described:

> vide sublime fusum, inmoderatum aethera,
> qui terram tenero circumiectu amplectitur?
> hunc summum habeto divum, hunc perhibeto Iovem (B. 43).

---

[75] References are to the *Phaenomena* (C. F. W. Mueller's Cicero, IV.3, Teubner 1879) unless otherwise specified. The same edition is used for all the *Aratea*. For other poems, Baehrens' *Fragmenta Poetarum Romanorum*.

[76] P. 32.

[77] Fr. 935 D.

There are *solis nitidos* . . . *ortus* (B. 19.8) in the *Ma-rius*, and *liquatae solis ardore* (B. 32.27) in a

Sun translation from Aeschylus; *clari solis* in 300.

The sun is often personified: *Titanum soboles* (B. 32); *Phoebi fax* (B. 3.20); *Titan* (294; 589); *laeti vestigia Solis* (339); *rota feruida Solis* (527); *Solis iter* (341); *convertit curriculum Sol* (510). It clothes the world and constellations with light:

> . . . perpetuo vestivit lumine Titan (294);
>
> haec Sol aeterno convestit lumine lustrans (578).

Moon An eclipse of the moon is referred to twice:

> cum claram speciem concreto lumine Luna
> abdidit et subito *stellanti* nocte perempta est (B. 3.19);
>
> cum neque caligans detersit sidera nubes
> nec pleno stellas superavit lumine Luna (490).

Stars Stars and comets in a prodigy are described:

> astrorum volucris . . . motus
> concursusque gravi stellarum ardore micantis
>
> . . . .
>
> . . . . et claro tremulos ardore cometas (B. 3.11).

Fixed stars are described:

> legitimo . . . caelum lustrantia cursu (469);

planets according to the idea of Aratus:

> quae faciunt vestigia cursu,
> non eodem semper spatio protrita teruntur.
> sic malunt errare vagae per nubila caeli,
> atque suos vario motu metirier orbes (472);

according to Cicero's own knowledge:

> stellarum motus cursusque vagantis
>
> . . . .
>
> quae verbo ac falsis Graiorum vocibus errant,
> re vera certo lapsu spatioque feruntur (B. 3.6).

Constellations are groups of stars.

> quas sideribus claris natura polivit
> et vario pinxit distinguens lumine formas (404).

Individual stars and constellations are variously described: The morning star is *praevius Aurorae; Solis noctisque satelles* (B. 1). Arcturus is

> stella micans radiis, Arcturus nomine claro (99).

The Pleiades are described:

> parvas Vergilias tenui cum luce videb;s (2C2).

They indicate changing seasons:

> hae tenues parvo labentes lumine lucent;
> at magnum nomen signi clarumque vocatu:
> propterea, quod et aestatis primordia clarat
> et post hiberni praepandens temporis ortus
> admonet, ut mandent·mortales semina terris (271).

The constellation Aquila (328), Arcturus and Ara (428), and, probably, Helice (38), are useful to sailors.

Constellations are sometimes described in terms applicable to the stars themselves. The crown:

> . . . illa eximio . . . fulgore Corona (73);

the kids with their dim light:

> . . . Haedi exiguum iaciunt mortalibus ignem (171);

Andromeda: *inlustri . . . corpore . . . Andromeda* (201); *sub pectore clarae Andromedae* (238); *Andromedae clarum caput* (361);

the horse:

> . . Equus ille iubam quatiens fulgore micanti (209);

the bowl: *fulgens Cratera* (463); the hare: *fulgentem leporem* (522);

the arrow: *clara sagitta* (724);

> hic missore vacans fulgens iacet una sagitta (325);

the eagle as if in flight:

> at propter se Aquila ardenti cum corpore portat
> igniferum mulcens tremebundis aethera pinnis (328);

Orion: *Orion claro corpore* (587); *claris cum lucibus enat Orion* (613);

> exinde Orion obliquo corpore nitens
> inferiora tenet truculenti corpora Tauri;
> quem qui suspiciens in caelum nocte serena
> late dispersum non viderit, haud ita vero
> cetera se speret cognoscere signa potesse (343);

the dog: *clari Canis vestigia* (382); *fervidus ille Canis* (715);

> rutilo cum lumine claret
> fervidus ille Canis (318);

the lyre: *clara Fides* (714); Hydra:

> longius exoritur iam claro corpore serpens (632);

the bird as in flight:

> quem rutila fulgens pluma praetervolat Ales (660).

Often the descriptive terms are applicable to the object from which the constellation takes its name. The dragon is *torvus Draco* in 47.

The bird is described:

> est Ales avis, lato sub tegmine caeli
> quae volat et serpens geminis secat aëra pinnis (231);
>
> . . . . nitens pinna convolvitur Ales (326);

the horse, *Equi vis* (291);

> clinata est ungula remens
> forti. Equi propter pinnati corporis alam (237);

the dolphin, *curvus Delphinus* (332);
the hare: *levipes Lepus* (365); the whale: *fera Pistrix* (384; 661). *Pistrix* . . . *caerula* (384); *caeruleam ferae caudam Pistricis* (521); *spinigeram caudam Pistricis* (422): the raven: *plumato corpore Corvus* (464).
The zodiac is:

> orbem signiferum. . . . . . .
> nam gerit hic volvens bis sex ardentia signa (564).

The signs of the zodiac are separately described. The crab: *claro conlucens lumine Cancer* (509):

> aestifer. . . pandens ferventia sidera Cancer (506):

the lion, *magnus Leo* (509); *fulgens.* . . *vis torva Leonis* (567);

> magnus Leo tremulam quatiens e corpore flammam (153);

the Virgin: *splendenti corpore Virgo* (101); *rutilo conlucens corpore Virgo* (568); *pandens inlustria lumina Virgo* (626); the scales: *claro cum lumine Chelae* (569); the scorpion: *Nepai fulgentis acumen* (427); *lucens vis magna Nepai* (570); the archer:

. . Sagittipotens dextra flexum tenet arcum (571);

Capricorn: *corpore semifero.* . . *Capricornus* (293); *ore fero Capricornus* (572); Aquarius: *radiantis Aquari* (416);

propter Aquarius obscurum dextra rigat amnem,
exiguo qui stellarum candore nitescit (417);

gelidum rivum Aquari (520); *umidus* . . . *Aquarius* (573); the fish: *squamoso corpore Pisces* (887); *squamigeri serpentes* . . . *Pisces* (574); the ram:

exin contortis Aries cum cornibus haeret (230);

Aries obscuro lumine labens (575); the bull: *truculenti corpora Tauri* (344); *inflexo genu proiecto corpore Taurus* (576);

corniger est valido conixus corpore Taurus (173);

the twins: *ora* . . . *Geminorum inlustria* (499); *Gemini clarum iactantes lucibus ignem* (577).

Epithets describing constellations and stars are: *aestifer* (*Cancer*, 566); *ardens* (*signum*, 565), (*Aquila*, 328); *clarus* (*sidus*, 404), (*Andromeda*, 238, 661), (*Canis*, 382), (*Navis*, 523), (*Scorpios*, 452), (*Orion*, 587, 613), (*Cheloe*, 569), (*Gemini*, 577), (*Hydra*, 612, 632), (*Fides*, 714), (*cometa*, B. 3.15); *conlucens* (*Virgo*, 568); *fervens* (*Cancer*, 566); *fervidus* (58), (*Canis*, 349, 715); *fugiens* (*signum*, 583); *fulgens* (*Sagitta*, 325), (*Nepa*, 427), (*Cratera*, 463), (*Lepus*, 522), (*Leo*, 567), (*Ales*, 660); *inlustris* (10 :70), (*Andromeda*, 201), (388), (*Gemini*, 499), (621), (*Virgo*, 626); *lucens* (*Nepa*, 570); *magnus* (*Leo*, 153, 509); *micans* (*Arcturus*, 99), (*Equus*, 209), (B. 3.12); *praeclarus* (*insignium*, *Arat. Incert.* 1), (*Deltoton* 243); *radians* (*sidus*, 59), (*Aquarius*, 416); *rutilus* (*Canis*, 345), (*Virgo*, 568), (*Ales*, 660); *splendens* (*Virgo*, 101).

Clouds Clouds are *oparem nubem* (445); and *caerulea nube* when the constellation Centaurus is described: *caerulea contectus nube feretur* (448).

Dawn   Dawn is:

    umida   .   .   Aurora   .   .

    .   .   .   .   clari praenuntia Solis (299).

Night   Night is *serenus* (345), and *stellans* (B. 3.19).
It is personified:

    non hiberna cito volvetur curriculo Nox (298);

    hoc spatium tranans caecis nox conficit umbris (584).

Wind   The north and south wind, especially the
former, often stand for the corresponding points of the
compass:

              Pistrix

    .   .   .   .   validas Aquilonis ad auras

    caerula vestigat finita in partibus Austri (385);

also 247; 256; 339; 341; 423; 498; 526.

The northwind is powerful, *validas Aquilonis* . . . .
auras (385), with whistling wings: *horrisonis Aquilonis*
. . . . *alis* (247); *clarisonis auris Aquilonis* (526). The
south wind is *validis* . . . *viribus Auster* (301); wind
upon the sea is described: *vehementi flamine ventus* (442), and
personified: *feras procellas* (444).

Sea   The constellation of Argo is compared to a
real ship:

    at Canis ad caudam serpens prolabitur Argo

    conversam prae se portans cum lumine puppim:

    non aliae naves ut in alto ponere proras

    ante solent rostro Neptunia prata secantes;

    sed conversa retro caeli se per loca portat.

    sicut, cum coeptant tutos contingere portus,

    obvertunt navem magno cum pondere nautae

    adversamque trahunt optata ad litora puppim,

    sic conversa vetus super aethera vertitur Argo (370).

A figure is found in a translation from Aeschylus[78] where
Prometheus is:

              religatum asperis

    vinctumque saxis, navem ut horrisono freto

    noctem paventes timidi adnectunt navitae (B. 32.3)

---

[78] Cf. Aesch. *frag.* 193.

The sea typifies disaster:

> nec tam aerumnoso navigassem salo (B. 42)

Is almost always referred to in connection with ships:

> hoc cave te in pontum studeas committere mense;
> nam non longinquum spatium labere diurnum,
> non hiberna cito volvetur curriculo nox.
> umida non sese vestris Aurora querellis
> ocius ostendet, clari praenuntia solis,
> at validis aequor pulsabit viribus Auster.
> tum fixum tremulo quatietur frigore corpus.
> sed tamen anni iam labuntur tempore toto,,
> nec cui signorum cedunt neque flamina vitant
> nec metuunt canos minitanti murmure fluctus (296).

Shipwreck is referred to *Arat. Incert.* 2.

Most often the dangers of the sea are referred to with the stars that guide or warn the sailor, as the bear:

> hac fidunt duce nocturna Phoenices in alto (40);

and the constellations Aquila and Centaurus;

> grave maestis
> ostendit nautis perturbans aequora signum (330):

> haec tamen aeterno invisens loca curriculo nox
> signa dedit nautis, cuncti quae noscere possent,
> conmiserans hominum metuendos undique casus.
> nam cum fulgentem cernes sine nubibus atris
> Aram sub media caeli regione locatam.
> a summa parte obscura caligine tectam,
> tum validis fugito devitans viribus Austrum;
> quem si prospiciens vitaveris omnia caute
> armamenta locans, tuto labere per undas;
> sin gravis inciderit vehementi flamine ventus,
> perfringet celsos defixo robore malos,
> ut res nulla feras possit mulcere procellas,
> ni parte ex Aquilonis opacam pellere nubem
> coeperit et subitis auris diduxerit Ara.

> sin umeros medio in caelo Centaurus habebit
> ipseque caerulea contectus nube feretur
> atque Aram tenui caligans vestiet umbra,
> ad signorum obitum vis est metuenda Favoni (133).

The signs which presage a storm at sea are described in the *Prognostica:*

> atque etiam ventos praemonstrat saepe futuros
> inflatum mare, cum subito penitusque tumescit,
> saxaque cana salis niveo spumata liquore
> tristificas certant Neptuno reddere voces,
> aut densus stridor cum celso e vertice montis
> ortus adaugescit scopulorum saepe repulsus.
> cana fulix itidem fugiens e gurgite ponti
> nuntiat horribilis clamans instare procellas
> haud modicos tremulo fundens e gutture cantus (*Prog.* 177).

The sea is: *altus* (10; 372); *caerulus* (B. 29. 3)); *canus* (305; *horrisonus* (*fretum.* B. 32. 3); *niveus* (*salis liquor*, *Prog.* 179); *vastus* (*gurges, Arat. Incert.* 3). The Aegean is mentioned, *Aegaeo gurgite* (674), and the Tyrrhenian sea B. 21. It is *Neptunia prata* (373), and is endowed with life in the expression *canos minitanti murmure fluctus* (305).

The constellation of the Dragon winds *veluti rapido cum*

Streams   *gurgite flumen* (46), and the cold stream of Aquarius is referred to, *gelido delapsum flumine fontis* (421); (cf. 520).

Hills are *celsus* (*celso e vertice montis Prog.* 181), (*excelsis*

Mountains   . . . *collibus*, 673), rocks *asperis saxis* (B. 32.2).

Flos is used metaphorically in *flore inventae* (B. 3.75).

Plants   The plane tree is *platano umbrifera* (B. 22.10,) and is again mentioned B. 22.13. The vine is described:

> bacchica quam viridi convestit tegmine vitis (675).

The effect of the dog-star on vegetation is described:

> hic ubi se pariter cum Sole in lumina caeli
> extulit, haud patitur foliorum tegmine frustra
> suspensos animos arbusta ornata tenere.
> nam quorum stirpis tellus amplexa prehendit,
> haec augens anima vitali flamine mulcet;
> at quorum nequeunt radices findere terras,
> denudat foliis ramos et cortice truncos (355).

The mastic tree is described:

> iam vero *semper viridis* semperque gravata
> lentiscus triplici solita grandescere fetu
> ter fruges fundens tria tempora monstrat arandi (*Prog.* 322).

Animals   Young birds are *teneros volucres* (B. 22.17) in
the translation from the *Iliad.* The eagle is *Iovis satelles*
(B. 32.12); *Iovis . . . pinnata satelles* (B. 19), and flies *prae-
petibus pinnis* (B. 19.9). The goat is referred to (*Arat. Incert.* 3). The most interesting bit of animal life is found
in the *Prognostica:*

> vos quoque signa videtis, aquai dulcis alumnae.
> cum clamore paratis inanes fundere voces
> absurdoque sono fontes et stagna cietis.
> saepe etiam pertriste canit de pectore carmen
> et matutinis acredula vocibus instat,
> vocibus instat et adsiduas iacit ore querellas,
> fuscaque non numquam cursans per litora cornix
> demersit caput et fluctum cervice recepit;
> mollipedesque boves spectantes lumina caeli
> naribus umiferum duxere ex aere sucum (*Prog.* 210).

Cattle are referred to, *vinctum domitumque iuvencum* (136),
and (*Prog.* 224).

The fact that almost all that remains of Cicero's poetry
is acknowledged translation, makes general
conclusions as to subject matter of little value.
Summary
In accordance with the nature of the Greek which he trans-
lated, phenomena of the heavens take the first place.

In the particular method of representing the phenomena
of nature, and in the epithets used, an independent treatment of some interest is found.

2. QUINTUS CICERO.

In Quintus Cicero's metrical descriptions of the signs of
the Zodiac, and other constellations, the characteristics of
the changing seasons are shown. The horns of Taurus are
"prophets of flowers," *florum-praenuntia*, (B; Quint. Cic. 3).
Pisces *flumina verna. . . cient* (1). Gemini *arida aestatis*

primordia pandunt (4).   Libra *Autumni reserat portas* (8).
The Scorpion, *ejetos ramos denudat* (10).   Sagittarius *pigra*
. . . *iaculatur frigora terris* (11).   Aquarius pours down
mists, *nebulas rorans liquor altus Aquari* (13).

Pisces is *obscuro lumine* (1); cancer is *praeclarus* (5); Leo,
ferus (6); the sun's "shining wheel," *rota fulgida* and the
moon, *Lunae simulacra*, pursue their course (15).

3. VARRO.[79]

The Menippean satires are the only poetical works of
Varro which remain.   Even in these the verse is mixed
with prose.   Yet, as the proportion of prose in the parts
that treat of nature is exceedingly small, the whole will be
considered together, without distinction.

The proportion of fragments dealing with nature out of
the whole five hundred and sixty, is about one-fifth.   A
very large proportion of these is concerned with animals,
but many interesting references to other forms of nature
also are found.

Sky
The sky is described in terms much like
those of Ennius, though no such extravagance
of metaphor appears.   It is *caelitum altum templum* (*Bimarc.*
XI), *caeli cavernas aureas* (*Marc.* IV), *caeli plagas* (*Lex. Maen.*
VI).

An eclipse of the moon occurs (KYNIΣTΩP I).   Her light
Moon
is once mentioned:

> candens corpore
> Taurus trivio lumine lunae (ΓNΩΘI Σ. VII)

and she is once personified:

> limbus . . . lunae bigas acceptat (*Dol. aut Ser.* I.3).

there are *vias stelligeras aetheris* (*Sesque.* VI).

---

[79] References are to *M. Terenti Varronis Saturaram Menippearum Reliquiae*, Riese, 1865.

Stars   Constellations appear in a simile:

ut sidera caeli
divum, circum terram atque axem
quae volvuntur motu orbito

(ΓΝΩΘΙ. Σ. VI),

and picturesquely in the following:

repente noctis circiter meridie,
cum pictus aër *feruidis* late ignibus
caeli chorean astricen ostenderet (*Marc.* III).

The zodiac is described in a passage which expresses a
sense of man's littleness amid the vastness of nature:

mundus domus est maxima homulli
quam quinque *altitonae* flammigerae
zonae cingunt, per quam limbus
bis sex signis stellumicantibus
aptus in obliquo aethere Lunae
bigas acceptat (*Dol. aut Ser.* I).

Clouds and Rain   Rain storms are three times described:

nec *coruscus* imber, *alto* nubilo cadens multus,
grandine implicatus *albo*

(ΤΡΙΟΔΙΤΗΣ Τ. V);

aut frigidos nimbos aquae caducitur ruentia (*Aeth.* I);

and more elaborately:

nubes *aquali*, frigido velo leves
caeli cavernas *aureas* subduxerant,
aquam vomentes inferam mortalibus (*Marc.* IV).

Dawn   The color of the dawn is referred to:

aurorae at *ostrinum* hic indutus supparum (*Eum.* XLI).

Night   Night is *niger*,

(de) nocte *nigra* ad lumina lampadis sequens (*Sexages.* XXI).

Wind and squalls are the subject of *Sesque.* IV, and *Herc.*
Tu. Fid. IV. The coldness of the north wind,
Wind   *aquiloniam frigedinem*, is shown *Cras. Cred. Hod.*
II, and hostile winds *Sesque* X.

4

The wind that bears the ship is compared to a horse:

> detis habenas animae *leni*
> dum nos ventus flamine *sudo*
> suavem ad patriam perducit

(ΚΟΣΜΟΤ. VIII),

and winds are personified:

> ventus buccas
> vehementiu' sufflare et calcar admovere (*Sesque.* VII);

> ventique frigido se ab axe eruperant,
> *phrenetici* septentrionum filii,
> secum ferentes tegulas, ramos, syrus (*Marc.* V).

Seasons   The four seasons are *anni tetrachordon* (*Serran.* II). Autumn is the season of Bacchus:

> cape hanc caducam Liberi mollem dapem,
> defrondem Bromiae autumnitatis uvidam! (*Quinquat.* VII).

Spring is characterized by the swallow:

> ver *blandum* viget arvis (et) adest hospes hirundo (*Incert.* XIII).

Sea   The sea is rarely mentioned except in connection with ships.
A few metaphors are taken from it:

> numve furentem eculum Damacrinum insanus equiso
> ex hibernis morbi educet fluctibus umquam? (*Eum.* XVII).

madness is *"pectore fluctuanti"* (*Eum.* XLVI).
The calm sea is shown:

> (albumst mare atque) adversi venti ceciderunt (*Sesque.* X).

Epithets of the sea often express color: *albus* (*Sesque.* X); *aquilus* (ΚΟΣΜΟΤ. VII); *caerulus* (*Marc.* II); *latus* (*Mod.* II).
The shore is shown: *per maritimas oras vagat* (*Herc. Tu. Fid.* III).

Ships are shown *Marc.* I; II; *Herc. Tu. Fid.* IV. A ship is compared to a water spider:

> ut levis tipulla lymphon frigidos transit lacus (*Bimarc.* XXI),

is *remivagam* (*Bimarc.* XX), *citiremen* (*Ag. Mod.* I), and figures
as a chariot (ΚΟΣΜΟΤ. VIII). The *phaselus* is its master's
delight:

> alius domini delicias phaselon aptum
> tonsil (lae de) litore mobile in fluentum
> solvit (*Desult.* II).

Streams   Streams are common. They are found in simile:

> *cavo* fonte uti cum inrigavit
> *cavata* amnium anfracta, in silvam volantes (*Parmen.* IV);

> uti rivus praecipitate in nemore deorsum
> rapitur atque offensus aliquo a scopulo lapidoso albicatur
> (*Cav. Can.* I);

metaphorically: *in reliquo corpore ab hoc fonte diffusast anima*
(*Andabat.* X), and *corporis fervidos fontium . . lacus
sanguinis* (ΠΕΡΙ ΕΞ. IV).

There is the stream that gives refreshment to the traveller: *retinet viatorem meridie praetereuntem fons, quod au-
tumnitas in anni tetrachordo mensum praeterierat* (*Serran.* II);

> Ismenias hic Thebagenes fluit scaturrex (*Est. Mod. Mat.* 6);

> Lydon fluens sub Sardibus flumen tulit
> aurum (ΕΚΑΤΟΜΒΗ I),

(cf. the Pactolus *Lex. Maen.* VII and the Albula
ΠΕΡΙΠΛΟΥΣ II).

To a stream is given the epithet *mobilis* (*fluentum,
Desult.* II).

Mountains   The usual dreary aspect of mountains is presented:

> Pieridum comes,
> quae tenet cava geloque acri (horrida) montium
> saxa (*Sesque.* XXII).

The mountains of Persia are mentioned (ΑΝΘΡΩΠ. II), and
the mountain regions of Scythia are described as inhabited
by "inhospitable solitude:"

> mortalis nemo exaudit, sed late incolens
> Scytharum inhospitalis campis vastitas (*Prom.* IV).

Woods   One figure is found:

> sum uti supernus cortex aut cacumina
> morientum in querqueto arborum aritudine (*Prom.* II).

There is a comic description of hunting (*Meleag.* II).
A grove is described:

> ubi lucus opacus, *teneris* fruticibus aptus (*Mut. Mul. Scab.* IV);

the lotus, olive and plane tree:

> caeditur lotos (atque) *alta* fros decidit
> Palladis platanus ramis (*Parm.* VIII, cf. IX),

and the fir:

> .   . alius *teneram* abietem solus percellit (*Parmen.* VII).

The common figurative use of good and bad harvests

Plants   occurs (*Lex. Moen.* IX), and the word *virgindemiam* designates a "harvest of blows" (*Agath.* VIII.5). Of frost the verb *subdealbare* is used (EXΩ ΞΕ. I). References to the earth and its products, in general unimportant, occur *Vinal.* I; *Ag. Mod.* III; *Flax.* I; ΓΕΡΟΝ. XI; XII; *Man.* XIII; ΓΑΦΗ ΜΕΝ. XVII.[30]

Flowers are mentioned only as a source of honey for bees (*Prom.* X, p. 141).

Birds are very prominent. They appear most commonly

Animals   in figures:

> natura humanis omnia sunt paria.
> qui pote plus, urget, piscis ut saepe minutos
> magnu' comest, ut avis enicat accipiter (*Marcop.* II).

A drinking cup is *nidus potilis* (*Quinquat.* VIII).
The swallow appears in a simile:

> ut hirundines virgultis oblitis luto tegulas fingebant
>
> (ΤΑΦΗ ΜΕΝ. XVI).

The swallow as harbinger of spring appears *Incert.* XIII, (p. 138); the owl, *formidant quam fullo ululam* (ΤΑΦΗ ΜΕΝ. III);
the stork:

> at nos caduci, naufragi, ut ciconiae;
> quarum bipinnis fulminis plumas vapor
> perussit, alte maesti in terram cecidimus (*Marc.* VI).

---

[30] Food plants are mentioned, *Long. Fug.* I; *Bimarc.* XXIV; *Eum.* XIV, XXVIII; *Man.* XVI.

Outside of figures appear: the young of birds, *pullas* . . .
fritinientes (*Virg. Div.* II);

> ad quos tum volucris venit pusillos
> usque ad limina nidica esca vilis (*Virg. Div.* V);

the kite, prophet of rain:

> iuget volitans miluus; aquam e nubibu' tortam
> indicat fore, ut tegillum pastor sibi sumat (*Sesque.* VIII);

the duck:

> nequiquam is *agilipennis* anates *tremipedas*,
> *buxeis* (cum) rostris pecudes, (in) paludibus
> (de) nocte nigra ad lumina lampadis sequens (*Sexages.* XXII);

the cock *Aborig.* I; ΟΝΟΣ Λ. II; *Eum.* XVIII;

the peacock:

> ut nitens pavoni' collus, nil extrinsecus sumens (*Sexages.* XXII;

ΓΕΡΟΝ. XIII.)

Of wild animals the variety is not great. The lion
(ΟΝΟΣ Λ. XI), wolf (*Sesque.* XI), hedgehog, and snake
(*Eum.* XVIII). The qualities of the fox are implied in the
verb *vulpinare* (*Mys.* III). The deer is most common. It
appears each time in connection with hunting:

> contra coactus cervu' latratu canum
> fertur bisulcis ungulis nitens humu (*Prans. Parat.* II);

> nempe (aut) suis silvaticos in montibus sectaris
> venabulo aut cervos, qui tibi mali nihil fecerunt,
> verrutis—ah artem praeclaram! (ΟΝΟΣ Λ. XX).

It is *cervum volabilem* (*Meleag.* VIII);
Other forms of animal life are: the bat, which belongs
"neither with mice nor with birds" (*Agath.* VII), the water-
spider (*tipulla, Bimarc.* XXI). Milesian bees: *quam apes
Milesiae coegerint ex omnibus floribus libantes* (*Prom.* X).
The crab, figuratively:

> ut in litore cancri digitis primoribus stare (*Armor. Jud.* II).

As in Lucilius, the horse is the most interesting of domestic animals, and is represented in various ways. Figuratively: *sed neque vetulus canterius quam novellus melior*

nec canitudini comes virtus, (*Aborig.* III). *Sed ut equus qui
ad vehendum est natus, tamen hic traditur magistro ut equiso
doceat tolutim* (ΤΡΙΟΔΙΤΗΣ T. III.). *Detis habenas animae leni*
(ΚΟΣΜΟΤ. 8, p. 138). The high spirit of the horse is prominent in the expressions *ecum mordacem calcitronemve* (*Sesque.*
XVII). Besides *ecus* and *eculus* is found *caballus* (*Sesque.*
XVI), and three colors are described: chestnut (*badius*),
pale yellow (*gilvus*), and mouse-color (*murinus*). (ΟΝΟΣ Λ.
XXI).

The dog is twice used in illustration: *ut canis sine coda*
(ΤΑΦΗ ΜΕΝ. IV);

<blockquote>sic canis fit e catello, sic e tritico spica (Sexages. X);</blockquote>

metaphorically: *quid latras, quid rabis* (*Id. At.* I). As in
Homer, the dog is the type of faithfulness (*Sesque.* 10). The
hunting dog appears (*Prans. Parat.* II). The forum is
satirically compared to a pigpen and the men busy in it to
pigs (*Prom.* XIII). Sheep are *lanigeras* (ΛΟΓΟΜΑΧ. I).

In Varro's satires, as in Lucilius', the animal world is
most conspicuous. As in Lucilius, too, many
references to animals (as well as to other forms
of nature), are made jestingly; unlike Lucilius, however,
Varro seems to take a real interest in them, and to
feel a certain human sympathy with them. This is
especially noticeable in the case of wild animals and
birds. Unlike Lucilius, too, Varro affords several interesting bits of description of other forms of nature, particularly of the stars, and of winds and rain. Epithets are
in general few, and are confined mostly to the sea. Color
terms, however, are used with comparative frequency.

Summary

Though the character of his works would seem least
adapted to encourage the expression of any deep feeling
for nature, it is not too much to assert for Varro a considerable interest in many of her manifestations.

Of a sympathetic relation between man and nature, no
traces are found, unless possibly in connection with the
animal world.

4. EGNATIUS.

Sky   Both fragments of Egnatius are concerned
with nature:

denique Mulciber ipse petens *altissima* caeli
continuo it (B. Eg. 1);

roscida noctivagis astris *labentibus* Phoebe
pulsa loco cessit concedens lucibus fratris (B. 2).

5. MARCUS FURIUS BIBACULUS.

Of the seventeen fragments of Bibaculus, only two represent nature. One is a mythological reference to dawn:

interea Oceani linquens Aurora cubile (B; M. F. Bibac. 8).

Another is a reference to snowy mountains,

Juppiter hibernas cana nive conspuit Alpes (B. 16).[81]

6. LUCRETIUS.[82]

A cursory reading of Lucretius leaves the impression
that there are many somewhat extended descriptions of
nature, both in connection with and apart from scientific
explanations of her phenomena. It is easy, however, to
over-estimate the quantity of descriptions, partly on account of the excellence of its quality; partly on account of
the frequency with which brief allusions occur throughout
the poems. By far the greater number of descriptions of
nature are used in illustration of the argument of the poem.
Sky   The sky is seldom used figuratively or in illustrations.

There are *caeli tempora* (I. 1066) for day and night; (V. 251,
VI. 362) for weather and seasons, *liquidissima caeli tempestas* (IV. 168) for fair weather. *Templa mentis* (V. 103) for
the mind involves a mixed metaphor, in its context, if the

---

[81] Cf. Hor. Sat. II. 5.41, for satiric mention of this expression.

[82] References are to Munro's edition (1593).

figurative force was felt. In a description of the effect of
superstition upon the mind, the figure used seems drawn
partly from the darkening of a stream with mud, partly
from the darkening of the sky with clouds.[53]

> funditus humanam qui vitam turbat ab imo
> omnia suffundens mortis nigrore neque ullam
> esse voluptatem liquidam puramque relinquit.   (III. 38).

In the illustration where the sky is used, as well as in
other representations of it, its grandeur and mystery are
made prominent.

To illustrate the point that no new thing is altogether
easy to understand, no familiar one difficult or marvellous,
the sky is used:

> suspicito caeli clarum puramque colorem,
> quaeque in se cohibet, palantia sidera passim,
> lunamque et solis praeclara luce nitorem;
> omnia quae nunc si primum mortalibus essent,
> ex inproviso si nunc obiecta repente,
> quid magis his rebus poterat mirabile dici
> aut minus ante quod auderent fore credere gentes?
> nil, ut opinor: ita haec species miranda fuisset.
> quam tibi iam nemo, fessus satiate videndi,
> suspicere in caeli dignatur lucida templa!   (II. 1030).

To show the impossibility of the existence of gods:

> quis regere immensi summam   . . .
>
> .   .   .   .
>
> quis pariter caelos omnis convertere et omnis
> ignibus aetheriis terras suffire feracis,
> omnibus inve locis esse omni tempore praesto,
> nubibus ut tenebras faciat caelique serena
> concutiat sonitu (II. 1097).

---

[53] The use of *funditus* and *turbo* seems to point to the former; *liquidus*
and *purus* are used both of water and sky, but mental conditions are so
very frequently compared by Lucretius to light and darkness that, even if
the first part of the figure here is drawn from a stream, it seems more
likely that the thought in the latter was of the darkening of the sky. Cf.
the description of the darkening sky, VI, 179; IV, 168 (p. 150). In the description of the formation of the world, V, 495 (p. 150), the sky itself is compared to the clear water left after the settling of mud:

and again to show why men suppose them to exist and
where:

> nam cum suspicimus magni caelestia mundi
> templa, super stellisque micantibus aethera fixum,
> et venit in mentem solis lunaeque viarum,
> tunc aliis oppressa malis in pectora cura
> illa quoque expergefactum caput erigere infit,
> nequae forte deum nobis inmensa potestas
> sit, vario motu quae candida sidera verset (V. 1204);
>
> in caeloque deum sedes et templa locarunt,
> per caelum volvi quia nox et luna videtur,
> luna dies et nox et noctis signa severa
> noctivagaeque faces caeli flammaeque volantes,
> nubila sol imbres nix venti fulmina grando
> et rapidi fremitus et murmura magna minarum (V. 1188).

The sky is:

> . . . . hoc, circum supraque quod omnem
> continet amplexu terram . . . . (V. 318),

and the same is said of the ether:

> qualis hic est, avido complexu quem tenet aether (II. 1066).

Many aspects are represented:
Its vastness is shown: *sublima caeli* (I. 340); *altum* (IV.
136); *altum caelum* (V. 446, VI. 287); *mundi magnum versatile
templum* (V. 1436); *alta caeli fulgentia templa* (V. 491); *caeli
impetus ingens* (V. 200); *patuli aequora mundi* (VI. 108);
prompta caeli (VI. 817); *magnus caeli orbis* (V. 510); *magni
caelestia mundi templa* (V. 1204) ; together with its hollow appearance, *caeli altus hiatus* (IV. 417); *magnas caeli cavernas*
(IV. 171); *aetheriis cavernis* (IV. 391); together with the stars:
signiferi orbis (V. 691); *signiferi aetheris aestus* (VI. 481); *stellis
fulgentibus apta . . . . caeli domus* (VI. 357); *stellis mi-
cantibus aethera fixum* (V. 1205). Its brightness and color:
caeli serena (II. 1100); *caeli lucida templa* (I. 1014; II. 1039) ;
fulgentia caelestia templa (VI. 387, cf. V. 491); *caeli clarum
purumque colorem* (II. 1030); *aera purum* (IV. 327); *caelo puro*
(VI. 400); *caeli caerula* (1. 1090); *magni caerula mundi* (V.
771); *caerula caeli* (VI. 96; 482); *caeli templa* is very com-

mon (I. 1064; II. 1001; VI. 286; 644, 1228); *caeli penetralia templa* (I. 1105); *Summania templa* (V. 521); *caelestia templa* (V. 1204; VI. 388; 670). *Caeli tegmen* is common (I. 992; II. 663; V. 1016); *caeli domus alta tecta* (II. 1110) carries the same idea. *Aetheris orae* is found (II. 1000; IV. 215;[84] V. 657; 683); with *altus* (III. 835; V. 143); *aetheriae orae* (V. 85; VI. 61); with *ingens* (IV. 411).

Epithets in the foregoing are: *altus* (II. 1110; III. 835; IV. 136, 417; V. 143; 446; 491; 584; 1434; VI. 287); *caerulus* (I. 1090; V. 771; VI. 96; 482); *clarus* (II. 1030); *fulgens* (V. 491; VI. 158); *ingens* (IV. 411; V. 200); *lucidus* (I. 1014; II. 1039); *magnus* (IV. 171; V. 510, 771; 1204; 1436); *serenus* (II. 1100); *signifer* (V. 691; VI. 481); *sublimus* (I. 340).

Sun   Figures are few. Its relation to the stars represents that of Epicurus to the rest of mankind:

> qui genus humanum ingenio superavit et omnis
> restinxit, stellas exortus ut aetherius sol (III. 1043; cf. III. 1),

and light is brought to darkness of the mind by philosophy:

> quo carmine demum
> clara tuae possim praepandere lumina menti,
> res quibus occultas penitus convisere possis (I. 143 .

So, too, philosophy is likened to the sunlight I. 146; II. 60; III. 91; VI. 40:

> hunc igitur terrorem animi tenebrasque necessest
> non radii solis nec lucida tela diei
> discutiant, sed naturae species ratioque.

Human life is represented as *lumina vitae* V. 989.

From the sun many illustrations are taken. The changes in the present forms of matter are illustrated:

> principio pars terrai nonnulla, perusta
> solibus adsiduis, multa pulsata pedum vi,
> pulveris exhalat nebulam nubesque volantis
> quas validi toto dispergunt aere venti (V. 251).

---

[84] *Luminis orae* occurs I. 22 (with *dius*), I. 170; 179; II. 577; V. 224; 781; 1155).

In the discussion of the reliability of the senses, the rising and setting of the sun at sea are used as illustrations:

> in pelago nautis ex undis ortus in undis
> sol fit uti videatur obire et condere lumen (IV. 432);

and a similar illustration is taken from the rising of the sun over a distant mountain (IV. 404). The swift motion of the atoms is illustrated from the sun as it suddenly fills the world with light on rising (II. 144, p. 151). Images in great numbers, all in an instant of time, fly from the surfaces of material objects,

> —quasi multa brevi spatio summittere debet
> lumina sol ut perpetuo sint omnia plena,
> sic ab rebus item simili ratione necessest
> temporis in puncto rerum simulacra ferantur (IV. 161).

The sun's heat and light are examples of the mobility of things made of very small atoms (IV. 185), and again, why should not the motion be swift, of images cast off from the surfaces of things, if atoms from within the bodies of things are swift?

> solis uti lux
> ac vapor, haec puncto cernuntur lapsa diei
> per totum caeli spatium diffundere sese
> perque volare mare ac terras caelumque rigare (IV. 200). [55]

Again they are:

> frigus ut a fluviis, calor ab sole aestus ab undis
> aequoris exesor moerorum litora circum (IV. 219).

Falling stars and the downward course of the sun's light illustrate the fact that no matter, of its own accord, can rise (II. 209).

Epithets of the sun are: *aetherius* (III. 1044; V. 215; 267; 281; 389); *praeclarus* (V. 120); *radiatus* (V. 462; 700); its light is *ardens* (*radius*, V. 755; VI. 860); *aureus* (*aurea matutina lumina*, V. 461); *candens* (*lumen*, V. 721; VI. 1197); *candidus* (V. 779); *clarus* (V. 779); *largus* (V. 281; 432); *liquidus*

---

[55] To illustrate the constant changes in matter almost the same words are used (V. 281).

(V. 281); *praeclarus* (*praeclara luce nitorem* II. 1032); *serenus* (II. 150); *splendidus* (II. 108); *tremulus* (*iubar* V. 697); the sun is figuratively represented as *radiatum insigne diei* (V. 700); *solis rota* . . . *altivolans* (V. 432); *solis rota* (V. 564); *sol rosea face* (V. 976); *sol rosea lampade* (V. 610); *aeternam lampada mundi* (V. 402); the sun and the light emanating from it are represented as a fountain:

> largus item liquidi fons luminis, aetherius sol,
> inrigat adsidue caelum candore recenti
> suppeditatque novo confestim lumine lumen (V. 281);

as a perfume:

> ignibus aetheriis terras suffire feracis (II. 1098);

as sowing the fields with light:

> sol etiam caeli de vertice dissipat omnis
> ardorem in partis et lumine conserit arva (II. 210).

The sun, moon and stars move across the sky like living beings:

> et solis flammam per caeli caerula pasci (I. 1090);
>
> solis . . varios cursus lunaeque meatus (V. 774);

(cf. I. 128; V. 76.)

and are further personalized:

> quove modo possent effecto lumine obire
> et neque opinantis tenebris obducere terras,
> cum quasi conivent et aperto lumine rursum
> omnia convisunt clara loca candida luce (V. 776);

as cherishing (*fovere*) plants and animals (I. 807); in the mythological account of Phaethon:

> solque cadenti
> obvius aeternam succepit lampada mundi (V. 401);

as teaching man:

> at vigiles mundi magnum versatile templum
> sol et luna suo lustrantes lumine circum
> perdocuere homines annorum tempora verti (V. 1436).

Moon   The moon, except in scientific explanation, is found only in the passages already quoted, where it is spoken of in a general way together with the sun. Its phases are *varias splendoris formas* (V. 716).

The stars are not often used in illustration.

Stars Their movements across the sky are often
represented. To show that nothing rises of its own accord,
it is said:

> nocturnasque faces caeli sublime volantis
> nonne vides longos flammarum ducere tractus
> in quascumque dedit partis natura meatum?
> non cadere in terram stellas et sidera cernis? (II. 206);

In the discussion of the reliability of the senses is found:

> raraque per caelum cum venti nubila portant
> tempore nocturno, tum splendida signa videntur
> labier adversum nimbos atque ire superne
> longe aliam in partem ac vera ratione feruntur (IV. 443);

and again:

> sidera cessare aetheriis adfixa cavernis
> cuncta videntur, et adsiduo sunt omnia motu,
> quandoquidem longos obitus exorta revisunt,
> cum permensa suo sunt caelum corpore claro (IV. 391).

Their reflection in water is shown (IV. 211, p. 162). Their
quivering motion is represented:

> atque ideo totum circum tremere aethera signis (I. 1039).

There are *palantia sidera* (II. 1031); *nocturnas faces caeli
sublime volantis* (II, 206); *noctivagae faces caeli flammaeque
volantes* (V. 1191); *aetheris ignes* (V. 448).

Epithets are: *candidus* (*sidus*, V. 1210); *clarus* (IV. 394);
fervidus (*signum*, V. 628, 642); *flammeus* (V. 525); *fulgens* (*stella*,
VI. 357); *gelidus* (VI. 720); *labens* (I. 2; *aetheris ignes*, I. 1034);
lucidus (*signum*, V. 518); *micans* (*stella*, V. 1205); *serenus*
(*serena sidera radiantia*, IV. 213); *severus* (*noctis signa severa*,
V. 1190); *splendidus* (*signum*, IV. 444).

They are invested with life (IV. 394); in *unde aether sidera
pascit* (I. 231); more fully:

> sive ipsi serpere possunt
> quo cuiusque cibus vocat atque invitat euntis,
> flammea per caelum pascentis copora passim (V. 523);

and in I. 1034, (*vivant*).

Clouds   Disease sweeps over the land like a cloud or mist (Vl. 1122). Dust is *nebulam nubesque volantis* (V. 253). Clouds appear generally in scientific explanations of their own nature and phenomena. They are used as illustrations but seldom. To explain the movements of planets:

> nonne vides etiam diversis nubila ventis
> diversas ire in partes inferna supernis (V. 646),

and the formation of "idols," spontaneously in the air:

> ut nubes facile interdum concrescere in alto
> cernimus et mundi speciem violare serenam
> aera mulcentes motu. nam saepe Gigantum
> ora volare videntur, et umbram ducere late,
> interdum magni montes avolsaque saxa
> montibus anteire et solem succedere praeter,
> inde alios trahere atque inducere belua nimbos (IV. 136).

The theory of images is again illustrated:

> praeterea modo cum fuit liquidissima caeli
> tempestas, perquam subito fit turbida foede,
> undique uti tenebras omnis Acherunta rearis
> liquisse et magnas caeli complesse cavernas.
> usque adeo taetra nimborum nocte coorta
> inpendent atrae formidinis ora superne (VI. 168);

and again by reflection of clouds (IV. 414, p. 162). Formation of clouds is described:

> praeterea fluviis ex omnibus et simul ipsa
> surgere de terra nebulas aestumque videmus,
> quae velut halitus hinc ita sursum expressa feruntur
> suffunduntque sua caelum caligine et altas
> sufficiunt nubis paulatim conveniundo;
> urget enim quoque signiferi super aetheris aestus
> et quasi densendo subtexit caerula nimbis (VI. 476).

Clouds when formed darken the sky (II. 1100), and, passing before the sun, cut the light off from the earth (V. 286). The brilliancy of rainless clouds is described:

> etenim cum sunt umore sine ullo,
> flammeus est plerumque colos et splendidus ollis (VI. 207).

Epithets applied to clouds are few: *aetherius* (IV. 182; 911; VI. 98); *altus* (VI. 479; 495; *altas nubis nimbosque volantis* VI. 484); *flammeus* (VI. 208); *furvus* (VI. 461); *niger* (VI. 256; 526); *splendidus* (VI. 208).

They are compared with other things apart from nature:

concipiunt etiam multum quoque saepe marinum
umorem, veluti pendentia vellera lanae,
cum supera magnum mare venti nubila portant (VI. 503).

They are in battle with the winds (VI. 98). Clouds when spread over the levels of the sky also give forth a sound,

carbasus ut quondam magnis intenta theatris
dat crepitum malos inter iactata trabesque (VI. 109).

They are compared with other phenomena of nature:

sunt etiam fluctus per nubila, qui quasi murmur
dant in frangendo graviter; quod item fit in altis
fluminibus magnoque mari, cum frangitur aestus (VI. 142).

There are mountains of cloud (VI. 159); caves:

tum poteris magnas moles cognoscere eorum
speluncasque velut saxis pendentibu' structas
cernere, quas venti cum tempestate coorta
complerunt, magno indignantur murmure clausi
nubibus in caveisque ferarum more minantur (VI. 194),

and a "night of cloud," *taetra nocte nimborum* (IV. 172).

Rainbow   In connection with clouds should be noticed the rainbow, which is mentioned only once in all the poetry of this period:

Tum color in nigris existit nubibus arqui (VI. 526).

Dawn   Dawn and sunrise are represented in their aspect on the earth:

primum aurora novo cum spargit lumine terras
et variae volucres nemora avia pervolitantes
aera per tenerum liquidis loca vocibus opplent (II. 144);

aurea cum primum gemmantis rore per herbas
matutina rubent radiati lumina solis
exhalantque lacus nebulam fluviique perennes,
ipsaque ut interdum tellus fumare videtur (V. 461);

in the sky:

> tempore item certo *roseam* Matuta per oras
> aetheris auroram differt et lumina pandit (V. 656);

nitor aurorae (IV. .538), is contrasted with the *nigror* of night.

Night   Darkness is used in illustrations:

> nam veluti pueri trepidant atque omnia caecis
> in tenebris metuunt, sic nos in luce timemus (III. 87; VI. 35).

Darkness stands for obscurity of life as opposed to fame:

> ante oculos illum esse potentem,
> illum aspectari, claro qui incedit honore,
> ipsi se in tenebris volvi caenoque queruntur (III. 75);

for intellectual difficulties:

> deinde quod obscura de re tam lucida pango
> carmina (I. 933; IV. 8);

for ignorance and misery:

> qualibus in tenebris vitae quantisque periclis
> degitur hoc aevi quodcumquest (II. 15);
>
> omnis cum in tenebris praesertim vita laboret (II. 54);
>
> e tenebris tantis tam clarum extollere lumen
> qui primus potuisti inlustrans commoda vitae (III. 1);
>
> quique per artem
> fluctibus e tantis vitam tantisque tenebris
> in tam tranquillo et tam clara luce locavit (V. 10);
>
> an, credo, in tenebris vita ac maerore iacebat,
> donec diluxit rerum genitalis origo (V. 171).

(cf. I. 1115; also I. 146; II. 60; III. 91; VI. 40, p. 146).

There are many allusions to the night sky and its stars: *noctis umbris* (V. 974), *nigrai noctis* (IV. 537), *noctes serenas* (I. 142), *severa silentia noctis* (IV. 460), *taetra nimborum nocte coorta* (IV. 172; VI. 253), *caeca nox* (I. 1115), *noctis caligine caeca* (IV. 456); *roriferis umbris* (VI. 864).

The sort of personification common in the tragedies, is

not found at all. The nearest approach to personification
is in the following:

> nec tibi caeca
> nox iter eripiet quin ultima naturai
> pervideas (I. 1115);
>
> nox ubi terribili terras caligine texit (VI. 852);
>
> hoc ubi roriferis terram nox obruit umbris (VI. 864).

The term *aura* is used for air (III. 400; 592; V. 236; VI. 1129);
and *aurae aeris* or *aeriae aurae* meaning air

Wind   occurs I. 207; 783; 801; 803; II. 203; III. 456;
570; IV. 933. The mind moves the body as the wind a
ship (IV. 897). Wind is figuratively used:

> . . . tu fac ne ventis verba profundam (IV. 931).

Winds are used in illustrations only a few times. Their
action helps explain that of " idols " upon the eye:

> ventus enim quoque paulatim cum verberat et cum
> acre fluit frigus, non privam quamque solemus
> particulam venti sentire et frigoris eius (IV. 259).

Thunder is sometimes caused by wind blowing through
clouds of irregular form:

> scilicet ut, crebram silvam cum flamina cauri
> perflant, dant sonitum frondes ramique fragorem.
> fit quoque ut interdum validi vis incita venti
> perscindat nubem perfringens impete recto.
> nam quid possit ibi flatus manifesta docet res,
> hic, ubi lenior est, in terra cum tamen alta
> arbusta evolvens radicibus haurit ab imis (VI. 135).

In the description of the seasons (V. 737 ff.), zephyrus is
one of the forerunners of spring, *etesia flabra aquilonum*
characterize summer (cf. VI. 720; 715), and autumn is ac-
companied by

> altitonans Volturnus et auster fulmine pollens (V. 745).

Favonus is typical of spring:

> et reserata viget genitabilis aura favoni (I. 11).

5

The power of wind is brought out:

> cur eadem credis sine corpore in aere aperto
> cum validis ventis aetatem degere posse? (III. 508);
> principio venti vis verberat incita portus
> ingentisque ruit navis et nubila differt,
> interdum rapido percurrens turbine campos
> arboribus magnis sternit montisque supremos
> silvifragis vexat flabris: ita perfurit acri
> cum fremitu saevitque minaci murmure ventus (I. 271),

(cf. I. 281, p. 160).

Epithets usually express strength and fierceness: *ferus* (VI. 592); *frigidus* (*vis*, VI. 319); *genitabilis* (*Favonus*, I. 11); *incertus* (*procella*, V. 504; 782); *magnus* (II. 766); *petulans* (*aura*, VI. 111); *rapidus* (*turbo*, I. 273; VI. 668); *saevus* (*procella*, III. 805; *tempestas*, VI. 458); *silvifragus* (*flabrum*, I. 275); *validus* (*auster*, I. 899; III. 494; 509; V. 254; 266; VI. 124; 137); *violens* (V. 1226; *turbo*, V. 217; 503; 1231); (*violentus turbo* V. 368); *volans* (*tempestas*, VI. 611).

Winds are personalized by the use of the epithets *saevus*, *validus*, etc., above, and more definitely, when they are compared to wild beasts (VI. 196 p. 151), and troops in battle:

> quod nisi respirent venti, vis nulla refrenet
> res neque ab exitio possit reprehendere euntis.
> nunc quia respirant alternis inque gravescunt
> et quasi collecti redeunt ceduntque repulsi (VI. 568),

(cf. the battle of winds and clouds VI. 97).

Rain and Snow. The downward motion of the atoms is compared to rain:

> imbris uti guttae, caderent per inane profundum (II. 222).

A shower of roses is compared to snow, II. 627, (p. 169).

Epithets of snow are *canus* (III. 21), *albus* (VI. 736) of melting snow on mountains; *gelidus* (VI. 107).

Seasons The changing seasons are noted:

> quod faciunt nobis annorum tempora, circum
> cum redeunt fetusque ferunt variosque lepores,
> nec tamen explemur vitai fructibus umquam (III. 1005),

and the atmospheric phenomena characteristic of them:

> fulmina postremo nix imbres nubila venti
> non nimis incertis fiunt in partibus anni (V. 675),

(see also I. 174; V. 670; 737.)

In spring, *tempora florentia veris* (VI. 359), thunder is frequent. Spring and autumn, when summer and winter are contending for mastery, are *freta anni* (VI. 374), and spring is typified by Venus, at the beginning of the first book. Summer is the season of ripening grain (I. 174); in autumn, the grapes mature (I. 174), and

> magis stellis fulgentibus apta
> concutitur caeli domus undique totaque tellus (VI. 357);

in winter :.

> cernis
> arbita puniceo fieri matura colore (V. 940).

The epithet *acer* is applied to winter (VI. 373).

Autumn is personified *autumno suadente* (I. 175), and all the seasons:

> it ver et Venus, et Veneris praenuntius ante
> pennatus graditur, zephyri vestigia propter
> Flora quibus mater praespargens ante viai
> cuncta coloribus egregiis et odoribus opplet.
> inde loci sequitur calor aridus et comes una
> pulverulenta Ceres et etesia flabra aquilonum.
> inde autumnus adit graditur simul Eubius Euan.
> inde aliae tempestates ventique secuntur,
> altitonans Volturnus et auster fulmine pollens.
> tandem bruma nives adfert pigrumque rigorem
> reddit: hiemps sequitur crepitans hanc dentibus algu (V. 737).

Sea   The sea is often figuratively used.
The epileptic

> agens animam spumat, quasi in aequore salso
> ventorum validis fervescunt viribus undae (III. 493).

The action of the magnet is caused by an air which

> trudit et inpellit, quasi navem velaque ventus (VI. 1033).

Atoms are themselves colorless, else why should the same objects so often change in color:

> ut mare, cum magni commorunt aequora venti,
> vertitur in canos candenti marmore fluctus (II. 766).

Atoms are infinite in number:

> —quasi naufragiis magnis multisque coortis
> disiectare solet magnum mare transtra guberna
> antemnas proram malos tonsasque natantis,
> per terrarum omnis oras fluitantia aplustra
> ut videantur et indicium mortalibus edant,
> infidi maris insidias virisque dolumque
> ut vitare velint, neve ullo tempore credant,
> subdola cum ridet placidi pellacia ponti,
> sic tibi si finita semel primordia quaedam
> constitues, aevom debebunt sparsa per omnem
> disiectare aestus diversi materiai,
> numquam in concilium ut possint compulsa coire (II. 552).

The newborn child lies naked on the ground

> . . . . . ut saevis proiectus ab undis
> navita (V. 222).

Metaphorically are found *maeriae tanto in pelago* (II. 550); a sea of trouble is expressed in *fluctibus e tantis* (V. 11); and the sea of life in

> idque minutatim vitam provexit in altum
> et belli magnos commovit funditus aestus (V. 1434).

spring and autumn are *fretus anni* (VI. 364; 374); there are *aerias undas* (II. 152) through which the sun's rays must make their way; *aetheris aestus* (V. 483; 519); and the air is compared to the sea in *mare acris* (V. 276) and *ventis furibundus fluctuet aer* (VI. 367). There are *belli fluctus* (V. 1289); *belli aestus* (V. 1435); *nigras lethargi undas* (III. 829); *mentis aestus* (III. 173), *curarum tristis in pectore fluctus* (VI. 34); waves of trouble (V. 11); of anger (VI. 74.)

The sea is used in many illustrations. Everything is produced from a definite seed; if it were not so

> cur homines tantos natura parare
> non potuit, pedibus qui pontum per vada possent
> transire et magnos manibus divellere montis? (I. 199).

Nature dissolves, but does not destroy, else

> unde mare ingenuei fontes externaque longe
> flumina suppeditant? (I. 230).

The movements of the ether are likened to the Pontus (V. 506). The invisibility of atoms is no proof of their non-existence:

> denique fluctifrago suspensa in litore vestes
> uvescunt, eaedem dispansae in sole serescunt.
> at neque quo pacto persederit umor aquai
> visumst nec rursum quo pacto fugerit aestu (I. 305).[66]

Almost the same illustration explains the formation of clouds (VI. 470). The theory of images, their exceeding fineness, is thus illustrated:

> denique in os salsi venit umor saepe saporis,
> cum mare versamur propter (IV. 222).

The production and sound of thunder is compared to the breaking of waves (VI. 142, p. 151).

From navigation many points are illustrated. The argument for the trustworthiness of the senses:

> qua vehimur navi, fertur, cum stare videtur;
> quae manet in statione, ea praeter creditur ire.
> et fugere ad puppim colles campique videntur
> quos agimus praeter navem velisque volamus (IV. 387);

> in pelago nautis ex undis ortus in undis
> sol fit uti videatur obire et condere lumen;
> quippe ubi nil aliud nisi aquam caelumque tuentur;
> ne leviter credas labefactari undique sensus.
> at maris ignaris in portu clauda videntur
> navigia aplustris fractis obnitier undae.
> nam quaecumque supra rorem salis edita pars est
> remorum, recta est, et recta superne guberna:
> quae demersa liquorem obeunt, refracta videntur
> omnia converti sursumque supina reverti
> et reflexa prope in summo fluitare liquore (IV. 432).

---

[66] For other aspects of the shore see p. 159.

The body is moved by the mind, a thin, invisible substance as the ship by the wind:

> quippe etenim ventus suptili corpore tenvis
> trudit agens magnam magno molimine navem
> et manus una regit quantovis impete euntem
> atque gubernaclum contorquet quolibet unum,
> multaque per trocleas et tympana pondere magno
> commovet atque levi sustollit machina nisu (IV. 901).

The same idea is found in a simile IV. 897.

The theory that color is not a property of atoms is illustrated from the whitening of the sea in foam:

> ut mare, cum magni commorunt aequora venti,
> vertitur in canos candenti marmore fluctus;
> .   .   .   .
> quod si caeruleis constarent aequora ponti
> seminibus, nullo possent albescere pacto (II. 766).

The stormy aspect of the sea is shown in other passages
as well as in some of the illustrations already quoted.

> nam fit ut interdum tamquam demissa columna
> in mare de caelo descendat, quam freta circum
> fervescunt graviter spirantibus incita flabris,
> et quaecumque in eo tum sint deprensa tumultu
> navigia in summum veniant vexata periclum.
> hoc fit ubi interdum non quit vis incita venti
> rumpere quam coepit nubem, sed deprimit, ut sit
> in mare de caelo tamquam demissa columna
> paulatim, quasi quid pugno bracchique superne
> coniectu trudatur et extendatur in undas;
> quam cum discidit, hinc prorumpitur in mare venti
> vis et fervorem mirum concinnat in undis;
> versabundus enim turbo descendit et illam
> deducit pariter lento cum corpore nubem;
> quam simul ac gravidam detrusit ad aequora ponti,
> ille in aquam subito totum se inmittit et omne
> excitat ingenti sonitu mare fervere cogens (VI. 426);
>
> summa etiam cum vis violenti per mare venti
> induperatorem classis super aequora verrit
> cum validis pariter legionibus atque elephantis,
> non divom pacem votis adit ac prece quaesit

ventorum pavidus paces animasque secundas,
nequiquam, quoniam violento turbine saepe
correptus nilo fertur minus ad vada leti? (V. 1226);

(cf. VI. 256). It hinders man by holding the lands apart.
(V. 203, p. 164.) Other aspects are shown in the following:
the surf on the shore:

insula . . . .
quam fluitans circum magnis anfractibus aequor
Ionium glaucis aspargit virus ab undis (I. 720);

the sea birds about the shore:

accipitres atque ossifragae mergique marinis
fluctibus in salso victum vitamque petentes (V. 1079);

the shells upon the beach:

concharumque genus parili ratione videmus
pingere telluris gremium, qua mollibus undis
litoris incurvi bibulam pavit aequor harenam (II. 374).

References to the sea in scientific explanations are found
VI. 552; 694; 890.

The sea is: *aequor* or *aequora ponti* (I. 8; II. 781; IV.
410; V. 1000; VI. 474; 628); *acerbus* (*Neptuni corpus acerbum*,
II. 472); *altus* (III. 784; 1030; V. 374; *gurges*, V. 387; 914 1434);
avidus (I. 1031); *caeruleus*, (II. 772); *caerulus* (*ponti plaga
caerula*, V. 481); *canus* (*canos fluctus candenti marmore* (II. 767);
glaucus (I. 719); *infidus* (II. 557); *immanis* (IV. 410); *immensus*
(II. 590); *liquidus* (*liquidam molem camposque natantis*, VI. 405;
1142); *magnus* (II. 1; 553; III. 1029; V. 270; VI. 144; 505,); 615
mollis (*unda*, II. 375); *naviger* (I. 3); *profundus* (V. 417);
rapidus (I. 720); *ridens* (*unda*, V. 1005); *saevus* (*unda* V. 222);
salsus (III. 493; 1031; V. 128; 482; 794; 1080; VI. 634; 891;
894); *sonorus* (V. 35); *subdolus* (II. 559; V. 1005); *turbidus*
(V. 1000).

The shore is: *bibulus* (*harena*, II. 376); *fluctifragus* (I.
305); *incurvus* (II. 376).

The sea is figuratively represented as a field; *campos natantis* (V. 488; VI. 405; 1142), *iam mare velivolis florebat pup-
pibus* (V. 1442); as *sudor maris* (II. 465), and by the term
velivolus (V. 1442) is implied an analogy with the sky. It

is endowed with life, by the use of the epithets *avidus* and
saevus, and in the description of its effects upon rocks and
walls:

> aestus ab undis
> aequoris exesor moerorum litora circum (IV. 219; cf. I. 326),

and more definitely personified, in the descriptions of its
cruelty and perfidy to man.   In the golden age,

> hic temere incassum frustra mare saepe coortum
> saevibat leviterque minas ponebat inanis,
> nec poterat quemquam placidi pellacia ponti
> subdola pellicere in fraudem ridentibus undis,
> improba naucleri ratio cum caeca iacebat (V. 1002),

(cf. II. 556).   This enemy Xerxes overcame:

> viam qui quondam per mare magnum
> stravit iterque dedit legionibus ire per altum
> ac pedibus salsas docuit superare lucunas
> et contempsit equis insultans murmura ponti (III. 1029).

Sailors wage war with the wind (IV. 968).

Streams   The most elaborate simile is that where the
force of wind is compared to a stream in flood:

> nec ratione fluunt alia stragemque propagant
> et cum mollis aquae fertur natura repente
> flumine abundanti, quam largis imbribus auget
> montibus ex altis magnus decursus aquai
> fragmina coniciens silvarum arbustaque tota,
> nec validi possunt pontes venientis aquai
> vim subitam tolerare: ita magno turbidus imbri
> molibus incurrit validis cum viribus amnis (I. 280).

The formation of the earth is compared to the settling
of mud in a stream or pond:

> Sic igitur terrae concreta corpore pondus
> constitit atque omnis mundi quasi limus in imum
> confluxit gravis et subsedit funditus ut faex;
> inde mare inde aer inde aether ignifer ipse
> corporibus liquidis sunt omnia pura relicta,
> et leviora aliis alia, et liquidissimus aether
> atque levissimus aerias super influit auras,
> nec liquidum corpus turbantibus aeris auris
> commiscet (V. 495).

The sun is several times compared to a fountain:

> illud item non est mirandum, qua ratione
> tantulus ille queat tantum sol mittere lumen,
> quod maria ac terras omnis caelumque rigando
> compleat et calido perfundat cuncta vapore.
> nam licet hinc mundi patefactum totius unum
> largifluum fontem scatere atque erumpere lumen,
> . . . .
> nonne vides etiam quam late parvus aquai
> prata riget fons interdum campisque redundet? (V. 592).

Figurative use of *rigare* and *inrigare* occurs also V. 281; IV. 203 of the sun; of sleep IV. 908; of the action of the will:

> principium dat et hinc motus per membra rigantur (II. 262).

Flow of language is compared to a full stream:

> hoc tibi de plano possum promittere, Memmi:
> usque adeo largos haustus e fontibu' magnis
> lingua meo suavis diti de pectore fundet (I. 411).

The magnet's power is regarded as a stream:

> inpellant ut eam Magnesia flumine saxa (VI. 1004).

There are also *sanguinis* . . . *calidum de pectore flumen* (II. 354), and rivers of odors:

> unde fluens volvat varius se fluctus odorum (IV. 675).

Fear of death is *fontem curarum* (III. 82). The verb *derivare* is figuratively used in the following:

> nec vitulorum aliae species per pabula laeta
> derivare queunt animum curaque levare (II. 364).

The constant dropping of water will wear away stone (IV. 1286).

The reliability of the senses is illustrated from a stream:

> denique ubi in medio nobis ecus acer obhaesit
> flumine et in rapidas amnis despeximus undas,
> stantis equi corpus transversum ferre videtur
> vis et in adversum flumen contrudere raptim,
> et quocumque oculos traiecimus omnia ferri
> et fluere adsimili nobis ratione videntur (IV. 420).

The explanation of images is illustrated from reflection in water (IV. 99), the argument for the reliability of the senses from the same:

> at conlectus aquae digitum non altior unum,
> qui lapides inter sistit per strata viarum,
> despectum praebet sub terras inpeto tanto,
> a terris quantum caeli patet altus hiatus;
> nubila dispicere et caelum ut videare videre
> corpora mirando sub terras abdita caelo (IV. 415).

The swiftness of the motion of images must be great:

> quod simul ac primum sub diu splendor aquai
> ponitur, extemplo caelo stellante serena
> sidera respondent in aqua radiantia mundi (IV. 211).

If living beings were on the other side of the earth they would be:

> ut per aquas quae nunc rerum simulacra videmus (I. 1060).

An explanation of the motion of the stars may be that an air flows below and moves them,

> ut fluvios versare rotas atque haustra videmus (V. 516).

The movement of images is *frigus ut a fluviis* (IV. 219; cf. IV. 675).

In addition to the foregoing aspects of streams there are streams flowing through level country:

> nec tenerae salices atque herbae rore vigentes
> fluminaque illa queunt summis labentia ripis
> oblectare animum subitamque avertere curam (II. 361);

mountain streams, *magnas e . . . montibus undas* (I. 1036), and streams in flood, (cf. I. 280, p. 160).

> nec tanto possent venientes opprimere imbri,
> flumina abundare ut facerent, camposque natare,
> si non extructis foret alte nubibus aether (VI. 266).

They are more picturesquely described in the following:

> et variae volucres, laetantia quae loca aquarum
> concelebrant circum ripas fontisque lacusque (II. 344),

and in the account of the primitive man:

> at sedare sitim fluvii fontesque vocabant,
> ut nunc montibus e magnis decursus aquai
> claru' citat late sitientia saecla ferarum.
>
> denique nota vagi silvestria templa tenebant
> nympharum, quibus e scibant umori' fluenta
> lubrica proluvie larga lavere umida saxa,
> umida saxa, super viridi stillantia musco,
> et partim plano scatere atque erumpere campo (V. 945).

The Nile is described in VI. 712.

Streams are represented by epithet as: *abundans* (I. 282); *altus* (VI. 143); *amoenus* (*fons*, IV. 1024); *gelidus* (VI. 1172); *largus* (*unda*, I. 1031); *lubricus* (*fluentum*, V. 949); *magnus* (I. 296; 1086); *perennis* (V. 463); *radens* (V. 256); *rapax* (I. 17; V. 341); *rapidus* (I. 15); (*unda*, I. 421); *validus* (IV. 291).

Streams are endowed with life in the following:

> ad caput amnibus omnis
> convenit, inde super terras fluit agmine dulci
> qua via secta semel liquido pede detulit undas (V. 270).

> et mora quae fluvios passim refrenat euntis (VI. 531);

ripas radentia flumina rodunt (V. 256), and also by the use of such epithets as *rapax* and *validus.* No more definite personalization is found, however.

There are mountains of cloud and hail (VI. 159). The

Mountains climbing of mountains illustrates difficulty in attainment and peace in attainment:

> ardua dum metuunt, amittunt vera viai (I. 659).

Epicurus

> et finem statuit cuppedinis atque timoris
> exposuitque bonum summum quo tendimus omnes (VI. 25),

and when the heights are reached there is peace; for

> —nil dulcius est, bene quam munita tenere
> edita doctrina sapientum templa serena,
> despicere unde queas alios passimque videre
> errare atque viam palantis quaerere vitae (II. 7).

A few illustrations only are taken from mountains.. Everything comes from a fixed seed, else why are there not men strong enough *magnos manibus divellere montis* (I. 201). In the argument for the trustworthiness of the senses, with many other illustrations from nature, occurs the following:

> exstantisque procul medio de gurgite montis
> classibus inter quos liber patet exitus ingens,
> insula coniunctis tamen ex his una videtur (IV. 397).

The constant change of material forms is illustrated by the wearing away of mountains:

> denique non monimenta virum dilapsa videmus
> quaerere proporro sibi sene senescere credas,
> non ruere avolsos silices e montibus altis (V. 311).

The invisible motion of atoms is illustrated from the appearance of a distant plain where soldiers are moving, from a hill:

> et tamen est quidam locus altis montibus unde
> stare videntur et in campis consistere fulgor (II. 331),

and of the hill from the plain (II. 317, p. 178).

The action of lightning upon dry clouds is likened to that of fire in laurel woods on mountains:

> aridior porro si nubes accipit ignem,
> uritur ingenti sonitu succensa repente;
> lauricomos ut si per montis flamma vagetur
> turbine ventorum comburens impete magno (VI. 150).

Mountains are useless to man and as such are classified with other useless regions:

> principio quantum caeli tegit impetus ingens,
> inde avidei partem montes silvaeque ferarum
> possedere, tenent rupes vastaeque paludes
> et mare quod late terrarum distinet oras (V. 200).

They are the home of wild beasts, to be avoided:

> ita ad satiatem terra ferarum
> nunc etiam scatit et trepido terrore repleta est
> per nemora ac montes magnos silvasque profundas
> quae loca vitandi plerumque est nostra potestas (V. 39)

cf. V. 824; 947).

Mountains and woods are the home of primitive man
(V. 955; 992); on mountains the trees, rubbing their
branches together, cause fire (I. 897); they are the home
of clouds (VI. 459), wind (VI. 469) and snow, (VI. 963).
Volcanoes are described in I. 722; II. 593; VI. 680.
A sense of the grandeur and peace of mountain regions
is felt in the following:

> inde minutatim dulcis didicere querellas,
> tibia quas fundit digitis pulsata canentum,
> avia per nemora ac silvus saltusque reperta,
> per loca pastorum deserta atque otia dia (V. 1384).

Probably *avia pieridum* (I. 926), refers to similar regions,
and the following, most distinctly of all, used to illustrate
the theory of sound:

> quo pacto per loca sola
> saxa paris formas verborum ex ordine reddant,
> palantis comites quom montis inter opacos
> quaerimus et magna dispersos voce ciemus.
> sex etiam aut septem loca vidi reddere vocis,
> unam cum iaceres: ita colles collibus ipsi
> verba repulsantes iterabant docta referri.
> haec loca capripedes satyros nymphasque tenere
> finitimi fingunt et faunos esse locuntur
> quorum noctivago strepitu ludoque iocanti
> adfirmant volgo taciturna silentia rumpi
> chordarumque sonos fieri dulcisque querellas,
> tibia quas fundit digitis pulsata canentum (IV. 573).

Mountains are described as: *altus* (I. 283; II. 331; IV. 1020;
V. 313; 492; 663; VI. 469; 733; 785; 963); *avidus* (V. 201);
cavus (V. 955); *magnus* (I. 201; 897; IV. 140; V. 41; 824; 946,
1244; VI. 191; 490; 786); *lauricomus* (VI. 152); *opacus* (IV.
573); *viridis* (*collis*, II. 322). There is a slight personalization in the expressions *avidei montes* (V. 201), and *lauricomos
montes* (VI. 152), and in the verbs *minari* and *furere* used of
Aetna (I. 722; II. 593).

Woods   Woods are not often even mentioned, and when
they are it is usually in connection with mountains, whither
man has driven them gradually by cultivation of the earth:

> inque dies magis in montem succedere silvas
> cogebant infraque locum concedere cultis (V. 1370).

Other passages referring to woods are I. 897; V. 41, 201;
955; 992.
In most of these passages they are shown as the home of
wild beasts, and as places to be avoided in general. In the
following a different aspect is shown:

> hinc laetas urbes pueris florere videmus
> frondiferasque novis avibus canere undique silvas (I. 255);
>
> et variae volucres . . . . . .
> . . . quae pervolgant nemora avia pervolitantes (II. 344),

(cf. V. 1386, p. 165).
Epithets are: *avius* (*nemus*, II. 346; V. 1386); *creber* (VI.
135); *frondifer* (I. 18; 256; II. 359); *ingens* (V. 1243); *profundus* (V. 41).
Laurel woods are the hair of mountains (VI. 152, p. 165).
Lucretius has much to say of the growth of plants and
Plants   the earth as the source of their growth. The
efficiency of the sun, so small a body, in lighting the whole
world, is illustrated from a burning grain field:

> quod genus interdum segetes stipulamque videmus
> accedere ex una scintilla incendia passim (V. 608).

The first growth of plants upon the earth is picturesquely described:

> principio genus herbarum viridemque nitorem
> terra dedit circum collis camposque per omnis,
> florida fulserunt viridanti prata colore (V. 783).

The earth and its fields are *daedalus* (*tellus*, I. 7; 228);
dulcis (*agellus*, V. 1367); *fecundus* (*gleba*, I. 211); *ferax* (II.
1098); *floridus* (*pratum*, V. 785); *frugifer* (*terra*, I. 3); *frugi-
ferens* (I. 3); *mollis*, (*arvum*, V. 780); *omniparens* (*terra*, II.

706); *virens* (*campus,* I. 18); *viridis* (*saltus,* II. 355; *nitor,* V. 783); *vividus* (*tellus,* I. 178).

Products of the earth are *frugiparus* (*fetus,* VI. 1); *laetificus* (*fetus,* I. 193); *laetus* (*pabulum,* I. 14; 257; II. 317; 364; 596; 675; 1159); *vineta* (II. 1157; V. 1372); *nitidus* (*fruges,* I. 252; II. 594; 994; 1157). Trees are *altus* (I. 897; II. 30; V. 935; 1393); (*arbusta,* VI. 140); *dulcis* (*pomum,* V. 1377); *laetus* (*arbusta,* II. 594; 699; 994; V. 921); *magnus* (I. 274); *glandifer* (*quercus,* V. 939); *tener* (*salices* II. 36).

Of other plants are the following: *teneras herbas* (I. 260), *viridantes herbas* (II. 33; V. 1396), *herbae rore vigentes* (II. 362), *herbae gemmantes rore recenti* (II. 319), *gramine molli* (II. 29; V. 1392).

The various sorts of cultivated trees in the country are shown (V. 1370, p. 185).

Plants are figuratively represented:

arboribusque datumst variis exinde per auras
crescendi magnum inmissis certamen habenis.
ut pluma atque pili primum saetaeque creantur
quadrupedum membris et corpore pennipotentum. (V. 786).

As instances of the effect of different kinds of atoms on the sense of taste are noted the *taetra absinthi natura ferique centauri* (II. 400) and the *amaror* of wormwood is referred to in VI. 929, and again in illustration of the argument:

praeterea quaecumque suo de corpore odorem
expirant acrem, panaces absinthia taetra
habrotonique graves et tristia centaurea (IV. 123);

That particles emitted from bodies act differently on different things is illustrated from the effect of plants on animals and man:

barbigeras oleaster eo iuvat usque capellas,
effluat ambrosius quasi vero, et nectare tinctus;
qua nil est homini quod amariu' frondeat esca.
denique amaracinum fugitat sus et timet omne
ungentum; nam saetigeris subus acre venenumst,
quod nos interdum tamquam recreare videtur (VI. 970).

Similarly, *cicuta,* is cited V. 899; *veratrum,* IV. 640.

The scent of nard is described:

> et nardi florem, nectar qui naribus halat (II. 848).

Things made up of rough atoms produce an unpleasant taste,

> faecula iam quo de genere est inulaeque sapores (II. 430).

The sound of burning laurel on the mountains illustrates that caused by lightning in a dry cloud:

> nec res ulla magis quam Phoebi Delphica laurus
> terribili sonitu flamma crepitante crematur (VI. 154).

The pear and arbutus were valued by primitive man:

> vel pretium, glandes atque arbita vel pira lecta (V. 965),

and the arbutus is characteristic of winter:

> . . et quae nunc hiberno tempore cernis
> arbita puniceo fieri matura coloro (V. 940).

Poppy seeds and ears of grain are typical of lightness and roughness respectively:

> namque papaveris aura potest suspensa levisque
> cogere ut ab summo tibi diffluat altus acervus;
> at contra lapidum conlectum spicarumque [84]
> noenu potest (III. 196).

Flowers play a very minor part. They are characteristic of spring (I. 8; V. 740), the rose in particular, (I. 174.) and flowers are figuratively used of poetry,

> iuvatque novos decerpere flores
> insignemque meo capiti petere inde coronam
> unde prius nulli velarint tempora musae (I. 923; IV. 3).

Flos is figuratively used of perfume, *nardi florem* (II. 848), of flame,

> donec flammai fulserunt flore coorto (I. 900, cf. IV. 450.)

of youth I. 564 (cf. *florere* IV. 450).

---

[84] Unless the metrical difficulty be considered insurmountable, Brieger's vindication of *spicarumque* (Burs-Jahresb. 1873), seems ample ground for retaining it.

Floridus is used literally of meadows (V. 785), figuratively,
novitas florida mundi (V. 943). *Florere*[87] is common:

> iam mare velivolis florebat puppibus (V. 1442).

florentia lumina flammis (IV. 450); also I. 124; 255; 1034;
III. 897; 1008; V. 329; 884; 888; 912; 1164; *florescere* is used
II. 74; V. 895. *Florifer* is literally used (*floriferis saltibus*
III. 11), and flower-sprinkled turf is described in II. 33.
The crocus' perfume is referred to in II. 416. Flowers
are *suavis* (I. 8). Showers of roses are compared to snow
in the account of the procession of Cybele:

> acre atque argento sternunt iter omne viarum
> largifica stipe ditantes ninguntque rosarum
> floribus umbrantes matrem comitumque catervas (II. 626).

Animals   The existence of animals hostile to man is
cited as an argument for the non-divine origin of the world:

> praeterea genus horriferum natura ferarum
> humanae genti infestum terraque marique
> cur alit atque auget? (V. 218),

and again the advantages that animals have in some ways
over man:

> at variae crescunt pecudes armenta feraeque
> nec crepitacillis opus est nec cuiquam adhibendast
> almae nutricis blanda atque infracta loquella
> nec varias quaerunt vestes pro tempore caeli,
> denique non armis opus est, non moenibus altis,
> qui sua tutentur, quando omnibus omnia large
> tellus ipsa parit naturaque daedala rerum (V. 228).

The exceeding fineness of " images," is illustrated from
minute living forms:

> primum animalia sunt iam partim tantula, quorum
> tertia pars nulla possit ratione videri.
> horum intestinum quodvis quale esse putandumst!
> quid cordis globus aut oculi? quid membra? quid artus?
> quantula sunt! quid praeterea primordia quaeque
> unde anima atque animi constet natura necessumst? (IV. 116).

---

[87] Serv. ad Aen. VII, 804 (*florentes aere catervae*) "Ennius et Lucretius
florere dicunt omne quod nitidum est."

6

It is not hard to understand how man developed language when we notice the elements of the same thing in
animals.

> cum pecudes mutae, cum denique saecla ferarum
> dissimilis soleant voces variasque ciere,
> cum metus aut dolor est et cum iam gaudia gliscunt(V. 1059).

So too necessity drove them to the use of language as it
drives animals to various actions:

> cornua nata prius vitulo quam frontibus extent,
> illis iratus petit atque infestus inurget.
> at catuli pantherarum scymnique leonum
> unguibus ac pedibus iam tum morsuque repugnant,
> vix etiam cum sunt dentes unguesque creati.
> alituum porro genus alis omne videmus
> fidere et a pinnis tremulum petere auxiliatum (V. 1034).

That the mind like the body springs from a fixed seed is
shown by the persistence of certain qualities in certain
animals:

> Denique cur acris violentia triste leonum
> seminium sequitur, volpes dolus, et fuga cervos,
> et iam cetera de genere hoc cur omnia membris
> ex ineunte aevo generascunt ingenioque,
> . . . .
> quod si immortalis foret [88] et mutare soleret
> corpora, permixtis animantes moribus essent,
> effugeret canis Hyrcano de semine saepe
> cornigeri incursum cervi tremeretque per auras
> aeris accipiter fugiens veniente columba (III. 741).

That the earth contains the elements of many different
things is certain,

> saepe itaque ex uno toudentes gramina campo
> lanigerae pecudes et equorum duellica proles
> buceriaeque greges eodem sub tegmine caeli
> ex unoque sitim sedantes flumine aquai
> dissimili vivont specie retinentque parentum
> naturam (II. 661).

_____

[88] vis animi.

Sentient beings are made up of senseless atoms,

> quippe videre licet vivos existere vermes
> stercore de taetro, putorem cum sibi nacta est
> intempestivis ex imbribus umida tellus;
> praeterea cunctas itidem res vertere sese.
> vertunt se fluvii frondes et pabula laeta
> in pecudes, vertunt pecudes in corpora nostra
> naturam, et nostro de corpore saepe ferarum
> augescunt vires et corpora pennipotentum (II. 871).

Plants and trees are *fetus* of the earth.

> sed genuit tellus eadem quae nunc alit ex se.
> praeterea nitidas fruges vinetaque laeta
> sponte sua primum mortalibus ipsa creavit,
> ipsa dedit dulcis fetus et pabula laeta (II. 1156).

The characteristics of animals are determined by the prevalence of one or another of the elements of the soul in their natures:

> quo genere in primis vis est violenta leonum
> pectora qui fremitu rumpunt plerumque gementes
> nec capere irarum fluctus in pectore possunt.
> at ventosa magis cervorum frigida mens est
> .   .   .   .
> at natura boum placido magis aere vivit,
> nec nimis irai fax umquam subdita percit
> fumida, suffundens caecae caliginis umbra,
> nec gelidis torpet telis perfixa pavoris (III. 296).

Different animals are attracted by different sorts of odors:

> ideoque per auras
> mellis apes quamvis longe ducuntur odore,
> volturiique cadaveribus. tum fissa ferarum
> ungula quo tulerit gressum promissa canum vis
> ducit, et humanum longe praesentit odorem
> Romulidarum arcis servator; candidus anser (IV. 679).

Animals know each other as men do (II. 349, p. 179).

The characteristics which protect different kinds of animals are shown in V. 866. Succession of generations among animals is likened to a race:

> et quasi cursores vitai lampada tradunt (II. 79).

Sentient beings arise from senseless atoms,

> quatenus in pullos animalis vertier ova
> cernimus alituum vermisque effervere, terram
> intempestivos quom putor cepit ob imbris,
> scire licet gigni posse ex non sensibu' sensus (II. 927).

The persistency of the markings of birds implies a basis
of indestructible atoms:

> . . variae volucres ut in ordine cunctae
> ostendant maculas generalis corpore inesse (I. 589).

Birds' feathers are used in an illustration in III. 386, (p. 174).

The notes of different birds under different circumstances
illustrate the development of human speech:

> postremo genus alituum variaeque volucres,
> accipitres atque ossifragae mergique marinis
> fluctibus in salso victum vitamque petentes,
> longe alias alio iaciunt in tempore voces,
> et quom de victu certant praedaeque repugnant.
> et partim mutant cum tempestatibus una
> raucisonos cantus, cornicum ut saecla vetusta
> corvorumque greges ubi aquam dicuntur et imbris
> poscere et interdum ventos aurasque vocare (V. 1078).

Birds are sympathetically described in the following account of the avernian regions:

> e regione ea quod loca cum venere volantes,
> remigi oblitae pennarum vela remittunt
> praecipitesque cadunt molli cervice profusae (VI. 742).

The song of birds is heard at dawn when

> aera per tenerum liquidis loca vocibus opplent (II. 146),

and it was from the song of birds that men learned the elements of music:

> at liquidas avium voces imitarier ore
> ante fuit multo quam levia carmina cantu
> concelebrare homines possent aurisque iuvare.   (V. 1379)

Birds announce the coming of spring:

> aeriae primum volucres, te, diva, tuumque
> significant initum perculsae corda tua vi (I. 12).

Birds are *genus alituum* V. 801; 1039; 1078; VI. 1216. They are *aerius* (I. 12; V. 825); *pennipotens* (II. 878; V. 789); *varius* (I. 589; II. 145; 344; V. 801; 1075); *varians* (*forma*, V. 825).

The fact that atoms are colorless is proved by the persistency of color in the raven and swan:

> conveniebat enim corvos quoque saepe volantis
> ex albis album pinnis iactare colorem,
> et nigros fieri nigro de semine cycnos
> aut alio quovis uno varioque colore (II. 822).

The raven and crow (*cornix*) are heralds of rain (V. 1084, p. 172). The swan is used in an illustration (II. 823) and is typical of the great, in contrast with the minor poet, (Epicurus and Lucretius), the latter represented by the swallow:

> . . quid enim contendat hirundo
> cycnis (III. 6).

and of literary work persuasive rather than copious:

> suavidicis potius quam multis versibus edam:
> parvus ut est cycni melior canor, ille gruum quam
> clamor in aetheriis dispersus nubibus austri (IV. 180, 910).

The swan's song is instanced with the lyre as the most musical of sounds:

> et cycnea mele Phoebeaque daedala chordis
> carmina consimili ratione oppressa silerent (II. 505),

and again in contrast with the trumpet:

> nec simili penetrant auris primordia forma,
> cum tuba depresso graviter sub murmure mugit
> et reboat raucum regio cita barbara bombum,
> et validis cycni torrentibus ex Heliconis
> cum liquidam tollunt lugubri voce querellam (IV. 544).

The hawk appears in an illustration (III. 752, p. 170), and in V. 1079, the quail (*coturnix*):

> praeterea nobis veratrum est acre venenum,
> at capris adipes et coturnicibus auget (IV. 640).

the vulture IV. 680, (p. 171); The crow *cornix* V. 1084, (p. 172); with the epithet *raucus* in VI. 751; the swallow,

hirundo, III. 6, (p. 173) crane, *grus* IV. 181; 910, (p. 173)
dove, *columba*, II. 801; III. 752, (p. 170) diver, *mergus*, gull,
ossifraga, V. 1079, (p. 172).

That atoms are themselves colorless is shown from the
changeable color of the plumage of the dove and peacock:

> pluma columbarum quo pacto in sole videtur,
> quae sita cervices circum collumque coronat;
> namque alias fit uti claro sit rubra pyropo,
> interdum quodam sensu fit uti videatur
> inter curalium viridis miscere zmaragdos.
> caudaque pavonis, larga cum luce repleta est,
> consimili mutat ratione obversa colores (II. 801).

The peacock is also:

> aurea pavonum ridenti imbuta lepore
> saecla (II. 502),

and is typical of beauty of color as in the same passage
the swan's song is typical of sweetness of sound.

To the goose is applied the epithet *candidus* (IV. 683,
p. 171,) and the cock inspiring terror in the lion is an
illustration of the fact that the same object has not the
same effect upon the sight of all animals:

> quin etiam gallum, noctem explaudentibus alis
> auroram clara consuetum voce vocare,
> noenu queunt rabidi contra constare leones
> inque tueri (IV. 710).

Images are very thin and easily unite with each other:

> tenvia, quae facile inter se iunguntur in auris,
> obvia cum veniunt, ut aranea bratteaque auri. (IV. 726),

and spiderwebs, with floating feathers and seeds, are types
of extreme minuteness, in the argument for the rarity of
the soul's atoms in the body:

> nam neque pulveris interdum sentimus adhaesum
> corpore nec membris incussam sidere cretam,
> nec nebulam noctu neque aranei tenvia fila
> obvia sentimus, quando obretimur euntes,
> nec supera caput eiusdem cecidisse vietam
> vestem nec plumas avium papposque volantis

qui nimia levitate cadunt plerumque gravatim,
nec repentis itum cuiusviscumque animantis
sentimus nec priva pedum vestigia quaeque,
corpore quae in nostro culices et cetera ponunt (III. 381).

The nature of images is illustrated from the cast off skins of cicadas and snakes:

ut olim
cum teretis ponunt tunicas aestate cicadae,
et vituli cum membranas de corpore summo
nascentes mittunt, et item cum lubrica serpens
exuit in spinis vestem; nam saepe videmus
illorum spoliis vepres volitantibus auctas (IV. 57).

Birds are described as originating spontaneously from eggs, in the early days of the world:

folliculos ut nunc teretis aestate cicadae
lincunt sponte sua victum vitamque petentes (V. 803).

Lucretius compares himself to a bee sipping the honey of Epicurus' works:

tuisque ex, inclute, chartis,
floriferis ut apes in saltibus omnia libant,
omnia nos itidem depascimur aurea dicta (III. 10).

The bee is again mentioned in IV. 679 (p. 171).

The apparent spontaneous generation of worms, is proof that sentient beings can be made up of non-sentient elements (II. 871; 899; 928; p. 171).

The passage of fish through the water illustrates the theory of void:

cedere squamigeris latices nitentibus aiunt
et liquidas aperire vias, quia post loca pisces
linquant quo possint cedentes confluere undae (I. 372).

They are *squamiger* (I. 162; 378; II. 1083); *mutae . . . natantes squamigerum pecudes* (II. 342); *squamigeris nitentibus* (I. 372).

A certain species of snake helps illustrate the principle that a substance harmless to one creature may harm another:

ut quod ali cibus est aliis fuat acre venenum,
extetque ut serpens, hominis quae tacta salivis
disperit ac sese, mandendo conficit ipsa (IV. 637).

The soul can not be immortal, since it can be divided, as we see it in the wounded snake:

> quin etim tibi si, lingua vibrante, micanti
> serpentis cauda e procero corpore, utrumque
> . . . .
> sit libitum in multas partis discidere ferro,
> omnia iam sorsum cernes ancisa recenti
> volnere tortari et terram conspargere tabo,
> ipsam seque retro partem petere ore priorem,
> volnoris ardenti ut morsu premat icta dolorem (III. 657).

If the soul were immortal, it would not complain at its dissolution,

> sed magis ire foras vestemque relinquere ut anguis (III. 614)
>   (cf. IV. 60).

The snake again is used in a figure (*lubrica serpens*), in IV. 60; (p. 175).

In the early days of the world, men

> per caelum solis volventia lustra
> volgivago vitam tractabant more ferarum (V. 931),

and they tried to use various animals in warfare, unsuccessfully, for they were intractable:

> nec poterant ullam partem redducere eorum;
> diffugiebat enim varium genus omne ferarum (V. 1337).

Wild animals are the enemies of man (V. 218; p. 169). In spring the spirits of animals awake with other things:

> inde ferae pecudes persultant pabula laeta
> et rapidos tranant amnis (I. 14).

but the most interesting representation is

> omne quod in magnis bacchatur montibu' passim (V. 824).

Wild animals are *fera saecla ferarum* (III. 753); *horrifer* (V. 218); *silvestria saecla ferarum* (V. 967), and *montivagus* (I. 404; *genus*, II. 597, 1081). The elephant is *anguimanus elephantos* (II. 537; V. 1303), *bos lucae* (V. 1302; 1339). The boar was one of the animals unsuccessfully tried in war, together with the lion,

> expertique sues sacros sunt mittere in hostis (V. 1309);

and the same two are named as objects of terror to primitive man:

> eiectique domo fugiebant saxea tecta
> *spumigeri* suis adventu validique leonis (V. 934).

The young of panthers are used in an illustration (V. 1036, p. 170), the panther as attacking human beings (IV. 1016). The wolf is characterized by treachery (III, 742; V. 863). Most conspicuous are the lion and the deer. Lions are used in illustrations (IV. 712, p. 174); V. 1036, p. 170); III. 741, p. 170; V. 862, cf. III. 741, p. 170).

They were tried in warfare:

> nequiquam, quoniam permixta caede calentes
> turbabant saevi nullo discrimine turmas:
> terrificas capitum quatientes undique cristas (V. 1313).

They are designated as, *acer* (*genus* V. 862); *fulvus* (V. 901); *rabidus* (IV. 712); *saevus*, (III. 306; IV. 1016; *saecla*, V. 862; 1313); *tristis* (*leonum seminium* III. 741); *validus* (V. 985; 1310); *violentus* (*vis*, III. 296).

The deer illustrates the effect of the prevalence of the element of wind in the soul (III. 299, p. 171). One must not believe that the gods draw souls down into the lower world:

> naribus alipedes ut cervi saepe putantur
> ducere de latebris serpentia saecla ferarum (VI. 765).

Deer are protected by their power of rapid flight (III. 742). They are *alipes* (VI. 765), and *corniger* (III. 751).

Domestic animals are conspicuous.

They are *laeta armenta* (II. 343), *mutae pecudes* (V. 1059), *variae pecudes* (V. 228). As wild animals have preserved their species through various inborn qualities, so certain forms have been preserved by the protection of man:

> Multaque tum interiisse animantum saecla necessest
> nec potuisse propagando procudere prolem.
> nam quaecumque vides vesci vitalibus auris,
> aut dolus aut virtus aut denique mobilitas est
> ex ineunte aevo genus id tutata reservans.
> multaque sunt, nobis ex utilitate sua quae

commendata manent, tutelae tradita nostrae.
principio genus acre leonum saevaque saecla
tutatast virtus, volpes dolus et fuga cervos.
at levisomna canum fido cum pectore corda
et genus omne quod est veterino semine partum
lanigeraeque simul pecudes et buccra saecla
omnia sunt hominum tutelae tradita, Memmi (V. 855).

Pasturing herds figure in the famous picture:

hinc fessae pecudes pingui per pabula laeta
corpora deponunt et candens lacteus umor
uberibus manat distentis hinc nova proles
artubus infirmis teneras lasciva per herbas
ludit lacte mero mentes perculsa novellas (I. 257).

In illustrations drawn from the effect of the same food
on different beings, the goat is found (IV. 642; V. 900;
VI. 970) and in the argument for variety in the shapes of
atoms:

praeterea teneri tremulis cum vocibus haedi
cornigeras norunt matres agnique petulci
balantum pecudes: ita quod natura reposcit,
ad sua quisque fere decurrunt ubera lactis (II. 367).

Epicurus is to Lucretius in genius, as the horse to the
kid in speed:

—quidnam tremulis facere artubus haedi
consimile in cursu possint et fortis equi vis? (III. 6).

The epithets used of goats are *barbiger* (V. 900; VI. 970);
corniger (II. 367); *tener* (II. 367).

Diseases of sheep and cattle are compared to those of
men, (VI. 1132; 1237). To explain the possibility of moving atoms in things apparently motionless, the sheep on
a hillside are instanced:

nam saepe in colli tondentes pabula laeta
lanigerae reptant pecudes quo quamque vocantes
invitant herbae gemmantes rore recenti,
et satiati agni ludunt blandeque coruscant;
omnia quae nobis longe confusa videntur
et velut in viridi candor consistere colli (II. 317).

The usual epithet of sheep is *laniger* (II. 318; 622; VI.
1237). There are also; *petulcus* of lambs, (II. 368); *balantum*

pecudes (II. 369); *pigris balantibus* (VI. 1132).   Cattle are
used in illustrations (III. 302, p. 171; IV. 60, p. 175; V. 1034,
p. 170).

The famous description of the cow seeking her calf illustrates the argument for diversity of shape in atoms:

> nam saepe ante deum vitulus delubra decora
> turicremas propter mactatus concidit aras
> sanguinis expirans calidum de pectore flumen;
> at mater viridis saltus orbata peragrans
> noscit humi pedibus vestigia pressa bisulcis,
> omnia convisens oculis loca si queat usquam
> conspicere amissum fetum, completque querellis
> frondiferum nemus absistens et crebra revisit
> ad stabulum desiderio perfixa iuvenci,
> nec tenerae salices atque herbae rore vigentes
> fluminaque illa queunt summis labentia ripis
> oblectare animum subitamque avertere curam,
> nec vitulorum aliae species per pabula laeta
> derivare queunt animum curaque levare:
> usque adeo quiddam proprium notumque requirit (II. 352).

The verb *mugire* is figuratively used:

> cum tuba depresso graviter sub murmure mugit (IV. 545).

Protelum is figuratively used:

> versibus ostendens corpuscula materiai
> ex infinito summam rerum usque tenere,
> undique protelo plagarum continuato (II. 529);

> suppeditatur enim confestim lumine lumen
> et quasi protelo stimulatur fulgere fulgur (IV. 189).

Bulls are among the animals tried in war (V. 1308).   Cattle are *bucera saecla* (V. 866; VI. 1237); *buceriae greges* (II.
663).   The pig is *saetiger* in an illustration (VI. 969, p. 167).

The sounds made by the horse under different circumstances illustrate the beginnings of language among men:

> denique non hinnitus item differre videtur,
> inter equas ubi equus florenti aetate iuvencus
> pinnigeri saevit calcaribus ictus amoris,
> et fremitum patulis ubi naribus edit ad arma,
> et cum sic alias concussis artibus hinnit (V. 1073).

To prove the necessity of the "swerve" in the motion of atoms, the race horse is cited:

> nonne vides etiam patefactis tempore puncto
> carceribus non posse tamen prorumpere equorum
> vim cupidam tam de subito quam mens avet ipsa? (II. 263).

The speed of the horse is brought out in III. 8, (p. 178). The verb *refrenare* is used figuratively (I. 850; II. 276; 283; 1121; V. 114; VI. 531, 568); *habenae*,

> quis regere immensi summam, quis habere profundi
> indu manu validas potis est moderanter habenas (II. 1095);
> arboribusque datumst variis exinde per auras
> crescendi magnum inmissis certamen habenis (V. 736).

The race horse is represented as even in sleep continuing the pursuits of his waking hours:

> quippe videbis equos fortis, cum membra iacebunt,
> in somnis sudare tamen spirareque semper
> et quasi de palma summas contendere viris,
> aut quasi carceribus patefactis (IV. 987),

and the nature of the horse is compared with that of man in the discussion of the centaur:

> principio circum tribus actis impiger annis
> floret ecus, puer hautquaquam: nam saepe etiam nunc
> ubera mammarum in somnis lactantia quaeret.
> post ubi ecum validae vires aetate senecta
> membraque deficiunt fugienti languida vita,
> tum demum puero illi aevo florente iuventas
> occipit (V. 883).

Horses are described as *acer* (IV. 420); *duellicus* (II. 662); *fortis* (IV. 987; *equi vis*, III. 8; 764).

The dog is perhaps the animal most sympathetically described. The origin of human speech is illustrated more fully from it than from any other animal:

> quippe etenim licet id rebus cognoscere apertis.
> inritata canum cum primum magna Molossum
> mollia ricta fremunt duros nudantia dentes,
> longe alio sonitu rabie restricta minatur,

et cum iam latrant et vocibus omnia complent.
et catulos blande cum lingua lambere temptant
aut ubi eos iactant pedibus morsuque petentes
suspensis teneros imitantur dentibus haustus,
longe alio pacto gannitu vocis adulant,
et cum deserti baubantur in aedibus aut cum
plorantis fugiunt summisso corpore plagas (V. 1062).

The discussion of the character of odors is illustrated from the hunting dog: (IV. 681, p. 171) and the deceptive quality of odors:

errant saepe canes itaque et vestigia quaerunt (IV. 705).

If everything did not come from a fixed seed,

effugeret canis Hyrcano de semine saepe
cornigeri incursum cervi tremeretque per auras
aeris accipiter fugiens veniente columba,
desiperent homines, sa perent fera saecla ferarum (III. 7

In the discussion of void is found the following simile:

multaque praeterea tibi possum commemorando
argumenta fidem dictis conradere nostris.
verum animo satis haec vestigia parva sagaci
sunt per quae possis cognoscere cetera tute.
namque canes ut montivagae persaepe ferai
naribus inveniunt intectas fronde quietes,
cum semel institerunt vestigia certa viai,
sic alid ex alio per te tute ipse videre
talibus in rebus poteris caecasque latebras
insinuare omnis et verum protrahere inde (I. 400).

The hunting dog is represented as hunting in sleep:

venantumque canes in molli saepe quiete
iactant crura tamen subito vocisque repente
mittunt et crebro reducunt naribus auras,
ut vestigia si teneant inventa ferarum,
expergefactique secuntur inania saepe
cervorum simulacra, fugae quasi dedita cernant,
donec discussis redeant erroribus ad se.
at consueta domi catulorum blanda propago
discutere et corpus de terra corripere instant
proinde quasi ignotas facies atque ora tuantur (IV. 991).

The faithfulness of dogs is shown in

> levisomna canum fido cum pectore corda (V. 864),

and *fida canum vis* (VI. 1222).

Summary   The greater part of Lucretius' references to nature are found either in purely scientific explanations, or in illustrating from common natural phenomena, philosophical theories or less common phenomena of nature. The first of these has been omitted in the present discussion, except where elements other than scientific are mingled with the science. These references to and descriptions of nature often reveal not only accurate knowledge but also a keen sense of the grandeur and beauty of nature. More illustrations are taken from the sun than from any other part of nature. Yet the sea furnishes almost as many, and owing to the way in which it is used, is on the whole more prominent. Lucretius groups sea, land and sky together as objects of interest to man, and implies but does not specify a choice among them

> et simul ac volumus nobis occurrit imago
> si mare, si terrast cordi, si denique caelum (IV. 732).

Of true similes not a very large number is found. The sun and the sea figure in the majority of these also.

Of metaphorical expressions, most are taken from the sea and streams. Epithets are abundant as regard number, but meagre in variety. Less than one-half are used but once of the same form of nature. About one-fourth are used of a given form of nature by Lucretius only.

The various manifestations of nature are not often personalized, with the exception of the sea, and the earth. Even the sun, so commonly personified by other poets, appears far oftener merely as a powerful source of heat and light than as "rolling with glowing chariot wheel," or "upholding rosy torch." Personalization of forms and forces of nature, especially such as verge on the mythological, would be foreign to Lucretius' grand conception of the universe, in which "Great Nature" ruled supreme.

"The idea which Lucretius revealed to the world in fuller majesty and life than any previous poet or philosopher, was the idea of nature apprehended not as an abstract conception, but as a power, omnipresent, creative, and regulative[89] throughout the great sphere of earth, sky and sea, and the innumerable varieties of individual existence . . . Nature is to him the one power, absolutely supreme and independent in the universe."[90] Above her, no power can even be conceived of: Nature is self-creative, self-controlling: "If, well considered, thou holdest fast to this, then does Nature seem, straightway set free, released from haughty lords, of herself, at her own will and through herself, to carry on all things, independent of the gods" (II. 1090). For "who is able to rule the vast universe, to hold and guide the strong reins of the great deep, who is able equally to turn the whole heavens, and warm with etherial fire the fruitful lands, to be present at all times, in all places?" (II. 1095.)

The control of nature extends over every detail of the universe. As no power is above her, so too no minor in-

---

[89] These attributes of life are brought out in the expressions *foedera natural* (I. 586; II. 302; V. 310; 924); *natura creatrix* (I. 629; II. 1117; V. 1362); *invida natura* (I. 321); *natura daedala rerum* (V. 234); and by very many verbs implying the action of living beings: *creare* (I. 56; II. 224; IV. 785); *alere* (I. 56; V. 220); *auctare* (I. 56); *resolvere* (I. 57); *parare* (I. 199; 551; IV. 785; VI. 31); *dissolvere* (I. 216; VI. 598); *pati* (I. 224); *reficere* (I. 263); *gerere* (I. 328; II. 242); *concedere* (I. 614); *tenere* (I. 1009); *cogere* (I. 1010; IV. 762; 812; 846; V. 831); *lutrare* (II. 17); *requirere* (II. 23); *dare* (II. 208; V. 180); *pascere* (II. 706); *reicere* (II. 714); *agere videtur* (II. 1090); *perducere* (II. 1117); *refrenare* (II. 1121); *ministrare* (II. 1142); *suppeditare* (III. 23); *mittere vocem* (III. 931); *intendere litem* (III. 950); *exponere* (III. 975); *coeptare* (IV. 405); *intersaepire* (IV. 918); *gubernare* (V. 77); *obducere* (V. 207); *parere* (V. 234); *removere* (V. 350); *convertere* (V. 811); *commutare* (V. 831); *absterrere* (V. 846); *tribuere* (V. 871); *redigere* (V. 877); *subigere* (V. 1028); *constituere* (VI. 226); *tollere* (VI. 470); *reddere* (VI. 608); *molliri* (VI. 646); *deferre* (VI. 1135).

[90] Sellar's *Roman Poets of the Augustan Age, Virgil*, p. 204.

dependent power exists beside her, but with direct control
she guides all things: "Moreover the courses of the sun,
and the wanderings of the moon will I set forth, by what
power nature guides them, lest perchance we think that
these, between heaven and earth, free, of their own accord
traverse their perennial course" (V. 76). Before the might
of nature man himself is powerless, and his appeals to gods
amid disasters are vain, "So ceaselessly does some hidden
force crush human fortunes, and seem to spurn and hold
in mockery the lordly rods, and the axes grim" (V. 1283).

The world is a vast organism, through which forever
work the powers of nature, which has brought it into being, controls it now, and will bring it sometime to an end.

The earth was evolved by nature from a chaos of disconnected atoms (V. 186). From it sprang plants (V. 783), animals (II. 1151; V. 791), and man himself (V. 805). The
earth, mother of all life, is still its support (II. 594; 991), but
her power is failing, she is not so fertile as once she was
(II. 1150). Moreover many forces are at strife among themselves and one day or another, some one will prevail over
the rest. In short, the "triple nature" of the sea and land
and sky, "one day will bring to destruction, and, sustained
through many years, the fabric and mechanism of the
world will fall in ruins" (V. 95). And after this will arise
"another and another frame of things," under the control-
ling power of "Natura Creatrix."

Such a view of nature it is fair to expect, will enhance
the author's appreciation of all forms of nature, and color
his treatment of detail. This great power, beyond and un-
heeding of man, must in every manifestation of itself reveal something of its own essence and energy, its grandeur
and sublimity, and rouse in its beholder feelings of wonder,
awe, and almost a religious reverence. And in general this
is the case, and these feelings toward nature are predomi-
nant in the poem. The life, power and energy of nature
are everywhere manifest. It is, as has often been remarked,

nature in action, rather than at rest, that is portrayed. All life, both vegetable and animal, interests Lucretius intensely.

The thunder, the earthquake, the volcano, the torrent, are described with power, even where the description is a part of a scientific explanation. The same tendency is evident in the epithets used of nature in brief incidental allusions.

Still, though it is the grand, and the fierce aspects of nature that prevail; and it is in these lines that Lucretius' genius is most remarkable, there is not lacking appreciation of calmer aspects and quiet beauties. This has already been shown in the discussion of the sea. Bits of vivid description, the whitening waves, the soft shell-covered beach, the swaying forest trees, a clouded mountain top, a dewy morning, flash before the eye. In this art of painting a landscape, denied to the Roman writers in general,[91] Lucretius is not altogether lacking, though where various forms of nature are put in juxtaposition, they are more often set forth in a disconnected series, than framed in one setting as an harmonious whole.

There are a few, but only a few, interesting pictures of the Italian country. Primitive man learned gradually to till the earth, and "they compelled forests to retreat to mountains, and the region below to yield to cultivation that they might have meadows, lakes, streams, harvestfields, and glad vineyards on hills and plains and that the dark sea-blue tint of olive groves parting them might run between their fields spreading over hills and vales and fields, as now you see graced with varied charms all the country which they plant and adorn with pleasant fruit trees and keep set roundabout with happy groves" (V. 1370).

The earth in the light of early morning is pictured.

[91] Friedländer, *Darstellungen aus der Sittengeschichte Roms*, Vol. II. p. 261.

7

The air of heaven was squeezed out from the earth in the
beginning, just as "when first the golden morning light
of the shining sun glows upon the grass begemmed with
dew, and ponds and over-flowing rivers exhale clouds, and
as the earth itself sometimes seems to smoke" (V. 461).

Scenes in which animal life appear are somewhat more
common. "When the dawn sheds fresh light upon the
earth and the various sorts of birds flitting through path-
less woods, through the tender air fill the place with
liquid notes, how suddenly the sun arising at such a time
is wont to clothe all things, bathing them with its light,
we see is clear to all" (II. 144). There is a picture of a
hilly pasture, "for often upon the hill cropping the glad
pasture, the woolly flocks stray slow, whithersoever
the grass begemmed with fresh dew calls and lures them
on, and the contented lambs frisk and playfully butt"
(II. 317). We are shown, too, the soft grass near a stream
of water beneath the branches of a tall tree where men
can enjoy themselves "without great wealth" (II. 29), and
where the early races of mankind found their happiness
(V. 1392). Yet this does not appeal to Lucretius as a picture, so much as it expresses a simple sensuous delight in
nature and her beauty. The same sort of appreciation appears from time to time throughout the descriptions of
the life of primitive man in the fifth book. The life then
lived was desirable in that it was simple, not, primarily,
in that it was close to the heart of nature.

Of the sympathetic or sentimental view of nature, there
seems to be little trace, here or elsewhere. The nearest
approach to this modern feeling is found in the appreciation shown for high mountain regions,[2] and in some de-

_____

[2] Only of these portions of the poem does Biese's assertion "ein deut-
licher Ansatz eines melancholisch idyllischen Gefühls für die Schönheit
der Natur, für ihre Stille und ihre Frieden im Gegensatz zu der ruhelosen,
Glück suchenden und . . . nie findenden Menschenwelt seiner Tage
giebt sich . . . zu erkennen" (p. 32), seem fully true. As has been
shown above, it is far oftener the stormy than the peaceful aspects of nature that appeal to Lucretius.

scriptions of the sea.   While nature herself is endowed
with life and power and almost human attributes, while
awe and wonder are shown in presence of her majesty,
there seems to be no attempt to endow her with a soul,
to find in her the reflex of human moods.   Lucretius' feeling toward nature, so far as it went, was akin to modern
nature-sentiment, but it stopped short of the highest point
that modern feeling has touched.

6.   GAIUS HELVIUS CINNA.[93]

Of the fourteen fragments, three refer to nature.   A
trace of the sympathetic conception appears in one:

> te matutinus flentem conspexit Eous
> et flentem paulo vidit post Hesperus idem (Cinn. 8).

Stars are *ignes aetherias* (11), a crystal is compared to snow.

> atque imitata nives lucens legitur crystallus (6).

Salicta are mentioned (1).
A picture of bright sails upon the topmast is found in the
Propempticon Pollionis (4), and another reference to navi-
gation in

> atque anquina regat stabilem fortissima cursum (5).

7.   GAIUS LICINIUS CALVUS.

In the twenty-one fragments few references to nature
are found.   The sun is personified (Lic. Calv. 13).   In the
Epithalamium,

> Vesper it ante iubar quatiens (5).

The country is *durum* . . . . *et laboriosum* (2).   If
Propertius 1.20.39 is modelled on Calvus and *lilium* should
be supplied before the words

> vaga candido
> nympha quod secet ungui (4),

Calvus is one of the few authors who mentions a flower
by name.

---

[93] References are to Baehrens' *Fragmenta Poetarum Romanorum*.

7. VERSES OF DOUBTFUL AUTHORSHIP.

The seventeen fragments assigned to this period furnish little material. One personifies the sun:

> hac qua sol vagus igneas habenas
> immittit propius volatque terrae. (Incert. 2).

The moon is personified:

> Luna, deum quae sola vides periuria volgi,
> seu Cretaea magis seu tu Dictynna vocaris (7).

The constellation of the bear is described:

> sed lucet in astris
> Calisto renovatque suos sine fluctibus ignes (6).

8. CATULLUS.[14]

In Catullus' poetry there are many references to nature, but none that reach a length of more than six lines, and only two as long as that.

The sky for itself alone is rarely mentioned. The night

Sky   sky is aetherias umbras (LXVI. 55), the clear sky aethera album (LXIII. 40); Jupiter is shown as pater divum templo in fulgente (LXIV. 387), and the expression in limine caeli (LXVI. 59) is found.

Sun   Days are reckoned by the rising and setting of the sun:

> soles occidere et redire possunt:
> nobis cum semel occidit brevis lux,
> nox est perpetua una dormienda (V. 4);
> fulsere quondam candidi tibi soles (VIII. 3, cf. VIII. 8).

and lux is found in CVII. 6 in the same sense as in V, 5.

The sun is represented as ardens (LXIV. 354); aureus (LXIII. 39); candidus (VIII. 3); clarus (LXVI. 44); flammeus (nitor, LXVI. 3); radians (LXIII. 39); rapidus (LXVI. 3); vagus (LXIV. 271). It is identified with day:

> ne qua femina pulchrior
> clarum ab Oceano diem
> viderit venientem (LXI. 88).

---

[14] References are to Ellis' Catullus, 1878.

It is personalized:

> progenies Thiae clara supervehitur (LXVI. 44);
>
> sed ubi oris aurei Sol radiantibus oculis
> lustravit aethera album, sola dura, mare ferum,
> pepulitque noctis umbras vegetis sonipedibus (LXIII. 39).

Moon The moon is mentioned as identical with Diana, in the ode to that goddess. She shines with borrowed light.

> tu potens trivia et notho es
> dicta lumine Luna. (XXXIV. 15),

and measures off the months:

> tu cursu, dea, menstruo
> metiens iter annuum,
> rustica agricolae bonis
> tecta frugibus exples (XXXIV. 17).

Stars The falling of the stars and change in their relative positions, is symbolical of the impossible:

> sidera corrurent utinam, coma regia fiam,
> proximus Hydrochoi fulgeret Oarion (LXVI. 93).

They are symbolic of countless multitude, like the sand, VII. 7; LXI. 205. They are called, together with the sun and moon, *omnia magni lumina mundi* (LXVI. 1), and their rising and setting by day and night (LXVI. 2) and at different seasons of the year,

> ut cedant certis sidera temporibus (LXVI.4),

are noted. They are *micantia sidera* (LXI. 212; LXIV. 206), and of individual constellations are shown *Virgo, saevi . . . Leonis lumina* (LXVI. 65), *Callisto, Lycaon, Bootes* (*tardus,* LXVI. 67), *Aquarius* and *Orion* (LXV. 94).

They are personalized: *reddita caelesti coetu* (LXVI. 37), and more fully:

> aut quam sidera multa, cum tacet nox,
> furtivos hominum vident amores (VII. 7).

Clouds Clouds together with winds are symbolic of inconstancy:

> tua dicta omnia factaque
> ventos irrita ferre ac nebulas aereas sinis (XXX. 11);

> haec mandata prius constanti mente tenentem
> Thesea ceu pulsae ventorum flamine nubes,
> aereum nivei montis liquere cacumen (LXIV. 238).

Mist symbolizes forgetfulness:

> ipse autem caeca mentem caligine Theseus
> consitus oblito dimisit pectore cuncta,
> quae mandata prius constanti mente tenebat (LXIV. 207).

Dawn Dawn is represented in connection with the sun:

> Aurora exoriente vagi sub limina Solis (LXIV. 271),

again LXIII. 39, p. 189, and with *purpurea luce* (LXIV. 275).
Night is *noctis umbras* (LXIII. 41); *caeca nocte* (LXVIII.
44); *aetherias umbras* (LXVI. 55), and is per-
Night sonalized, *cum tacet nox* (VII. 7); *vaga nocte*
(LXI. 117).

The wind is very frequently used figuratively. For
greed: *turbida rapacior procella* (XXV. 4). For
Winds fleetness together with horses and birds:

> non custos si fingar ille Cretum,
> non si Pegaseo ferar volatu,
> non Ladas ego pinnipesve Perseus,
> non Rhesi niveae citaeque bigae;
> adde huc plumipedas volatilesque,
> ventorumque simul require cursum,
> quos iunctos, Cameri, mihi dicares (LV. 15);

for inconstancy. Theseus leaves Ariadne:

> irrita ventosae linquens promissa procellae (LXIV. 59).

Again Ariadne laments his promises:

> quae cuncta aerei discerpunt irrita venti (LXIV. 142).

Catullus sends his poem to his friend in accordance with
his request:

> ne tua dicta vagis nequicquam credita ventis
> effluxisse meo forte putes animo (LXV. 17),

and complains of Lesbia:

> . . . mulier cupido quod dicit amanti,
> in vento et rapida scribere oportet aqua (LXX. 3).

Auster, Favonus, Boreas, and the Apheliotes appear in the pun on the mortgaged villa (XXVI).

Epithets, of which those expressing mildness are the commonest, are *aereus* (LXIV. 142); *clemens* (*Zephyrus*, LXIV. 272); *fecundus* (*Favonus*, LXIV. 282); *iocundus* (*Zephyrus*, XLVI. 3); *lenis* (*aura*, LXIV. 84); *levis* (*flamen*, LXIV. 9); *niger* (*turbo*, LXVIII. 65); *saevus* (*Boreas*, XXVI. 3); *tepidus* (*Favonus*, LXIV. 282); *turbidus* (*procella*, XXV. 4); *vagus* (LXV. 17); *ventosus* (LXIV. 59); *vernus* (*aura*, LXIV. 90).

Winds are partially personalized in the use of the epithet *saevus* of *Boreas* (XXVI. 3); the verb *vesanire* (XXV. 13); in the following:

> (flos)—quem mulcent aurae (LXII. 50)
>
> .   .   .   .   .   laeva sive dextera
> vocaret aura   .   .   .   (IV. 19)

(cf. LXIV. 213); and more distinctly in

> sed quid ego ignaris nequicquam conquerar auris,
> externata malo, quae nullis sensibus auctae
> nec missas audire queunt nec reddere voces (LXIV. 164).

Tears are rain, *tristique imbre madere genae* (LXVIII. 58);

Rain and Snow Rain calls forth the flowers (LXII. 50). The adjective *niveus* is used, (LV. 18; LXIII. 8; LXIV. 364; LXVIII. 127; *candidior nive* is found in LXXX. 2.

Seasons Youth is typified by spring:

> iucundum cum aetas florida ver ageret (LXVIII. 16).

and spring is described:

> iam ver egelidos refert tepores,
> iam caeli furor aequinoctialis
> iocundis Zephyri silescit aureis (XLVI. 1).

Winter and summer measure time.

> .   .   .   .   .   nonam post denique messem
> .   .   nonamque   .   .   post hiemem (XCV. 2).

Sea   The sea is very often used in similes:

> et insolenter aestues, velut minuta magno
> deprensa navis in mari, vesaniente vento (XXV. 12).

A person in trouble is compared to a shipwrecked sailor:

> conscriptum hoc lacrimis mittis epistolium,
> naufragum ut eiectum spumantibus aequoris undis
> sublevem et a mortis limine restituam (LXVIII. 2);

> hic, velut in nigro iactatis turbine nautis
> lenius aspirans aura secunda venit
> iam prece Pollucis, iam Castoris implorata,
> tale fuit nobis Mallius auxilium (LXVIII. 65).

The most elaborate simile is that where the guests de-
parting from the wedding of Peleus and Thetis are compared to the waves of the sea, increasing as the wind
freshens:

> hic, qualis flatu placidum mare matutino
> horrificans Zephyrus proclivas incitat undas,
> Aurora exoriente vagi sub limina Solis,
> quae tarde primum clementi flamine pulsae
> procedunt, leviter resonant plangore cachinni,
> post vento crescente magis magis increbescunt,
> purpureaque procul nautes ab luce refulgent;
> sic tum vestibuli linquentis regia tecta
> at se quisque vago passim pede discedebant (LXIV. 269).

In metaphor, it is used of death:

> certe ego te in medio versantem turbine leti. (LXIV. 149);

For mental trouble:

> animo aestuante rusum reditum ad vada tetulit (LXIII. 47);
> prospicit et magnis curarum fluctuat undis (LXIV. 62);
> qualibus incensam iactastis mente puellam
> fluctibus (LXIV. 97).

Catullus says of himself:

> mens animi, tantis fluctuat ipsa malis (LXV. 4);
> accipe, quis merser fortunae fluctibus ipse (LXVIII. 13).

The voyage of the Argo is described:

> ausi sunt vada salsa cita decurrere puppi,
> caerula verrentes abiegnis aequora palmis (LXIV. 6).

Catullus is especially rich in epithets for the sea of which the commonest are those representing its motion, often in storm. There are *altus* (LXIII. 1; LXVI. 68); *caeruleus* (XXXVI. 11); *caerulus* (LXIV. 7); *candens* (LXIV. 14); *canus* (LXIV. 18); *ferus* (LXIII. 40); *horridus* (LXIV. 205); *impotens* (IV. 18); *latus (gurges,* LXIV. 178); *liquidus (unda,* LXIV. 2); *magnus* (XXV. 12); *minax (Adriaticus,* IV. 6); *placidus* (LXIV. 269); *proclivus (unda,* LXIV. 270); *rapidus (salum,* LXIII. 16; *Hellespontus,* LXIV, 358); *salsus* (and *sal*) (LXIV. 6; 67; 128); *spumans (unda,* LXIV. 155; LXVIII. 3); *tremulus* (LXIV. 128); *truculentus* (LXIII. 16; LXIV. 179); *trux* (IV. 9); *vastus* (XXXI. 3; LXIII. 48; *pelagi aestus,* LXIV. 127); *ventosus* (LXIV. 12).

The shore is *curvus* (LXIV. 74); *desertus* (LXIV. 133); *fluentisonus* (LXIV. 52); *spumosus* (LXIV. 121); *vacuus (alga,* LXIV. 168). The sea is also called *marmor pelagei* (LXIII. 88). The verb *volare* is used of the boat upon the sea (IV. 5). The sea is personalized by the use of such epithets as *minax,* quoted above, and, as the embodiment of cruelty:

quaenam te genuit sola sub rupe leaena,
quod mare conceptum spumantibus expuit undis (LXIV. 154);

mythologically as *Tethys* and *Oceanus* (LXIV. 29; LXXXVIII, 5); as *Amphitrite* in LXIV. 11.

A boat is represented as a living being by the terms *volare* (IV. 5), *senere* (IV. 26), and indeed throughout the fourth poem.

Streams   One simile is found:

qualis in aerei perlucens vertice montis
rivus muscoso prosilit e lapide,
qui cum de prona praeceps est valle volutus,
per medium densi transit iter populi,
dulce viatori lasso in sudore levamen,
cum gravis exustos aestus biulcat agros (LXVIII. 59);

such was Mallius to his friend in trouble. Metaphorically, boiling springs represent the fire of love (LXVIII. 56).

Diana is *domina* . . . *amnium sonantum* (XXXIV. 12);
rapidus is used of water in (LXX. 4, p. 191).

Individual rivers are the Nile: *quae septemgeminus colorat
aequora Nilus* (XI. 7); the Scamander:

> testis erit magnis virtutibus unda Scamandri,
> quae passim rapido diffunditur Hellesponto,
> cuius iter caesis angustans corporum acervis
> *alta* tepefaciet permixta flumina caede (LXIV. 357);

the fountain Aganippe:

> rupis Aonios specus,
> nympha quos super irrigat
> *frigerans* Aganippe (LXI. 28);

Gallicum Rhenum (XI 11), and *aurifer Tagus* (XXIX. 19).

Lakes In the account of the phaselus, the lake is *limpidum lacum* (IV. 24). In the Sirmio it is *liquentibus stagnis* (XXXI. 2), and the island and lake are addressed:

> salve o venusta Sirmio atque hero gaude;
> gaudete vosque o Lydiae lacus undae;
> ridete quicquid est domi cachinnorum (XXXI. 12).

Mountains Mount Aetna is used in a simile for the fire of love:

> cum tantum arderem quantum Trinacria rupes (LXVIII. 55).

The dreary aspect of mountains is usually presented:

> ad Idae tetuli nemora pedem,
> ut aput nivem et ferarum gelida stabula forem (LXIII. 52);

> ego viridis algida Idae nive amicta loca colam?
> ego vitam agam sub altis Phrygiae columinibus,
> ubi cerva silvicultrix, ubi aper nemorivagus? (LXIII. 70).

Thrace is *horridam Thraciam* (IV. 8). Only once is a pleasanter aspect shown:

> montium domina ut fores
> silvarumque virentium
> saltuumque reconditorum
> amniumque sonantum (XXXIV. 9).

Epithets of mountains are varied: *aereus* (LXIV. 240; LXVIII. 59); *algidus* (LXIII. 70); *altus* (*Alpes*, XI. 9); *buxifer*

(Cytorus, IV. 13); *frondosus (Idalium,* LXIV. 96); *gelidus (stabula ferarum,* LXIII. 53); *magnus* (LXIV. 280); *niveus* (LXIV. 240); *praeruptus* (LXIV. 126) ; *viridis (Ida,* LXIII. 70). The one figurative representation is "columns of Phrygia" (LXIII. 71).

Woods   Woods generally appear in connection with mountains, as in LXIII. 12; 52.

Tempe is described:

viridantia Tempe,
Tempe, quae silvae cingunt super impendentes (LXIV. 285).

They are *altus* (LXIII. 12); *ferus* (LXIII. 89); *opacus* (LXIII. 3; 32); *virens* (XXXIV. 10).

They are personalized:

ubi iste post phasellus antea fuit
comata silva: nam Cytorio in iugo
loquente saepe sibilum edidit coma (IV. 10).

Plants are very commonly used in similes. The mino-
Plants   taur falls like an oak or pine on the mountain:

Nam velut in summo quatientem brachia Tauro
quercum, aut *conigeram sudanti cortice* pinum,
indomitus turbo contorquens flamine robur,
eruit (illa procul radicitus exturbata
prona cadit, lateque et cominus obvia frangens),
sic domito saevum prostravit corpore Theseus
nequicquam vanis iactantem cornua ventis (LXIV. 105).

The vine and tree are found:

mentem amore revinciens
ut *tenax* edera huc et huc
arborem implicat errans (LXI. 33).

Flowers are conspicuous. The young girl is:

ut flos in septis secretus nascitur hortis,
ignotus pecori, nullo contusus aratro,
quem mulcent aurae, firmat sol, educat imber (LXII. 48).

Ariadne is reared in her home,

quales Eurotae progignunt flumina myrtus,
auraeve distinctos educit verna colores (LXIV. 89).

Vinia is compared to the larkspur:

> talis in vario solet
> divitis domini hortulo
> stare flos hyacinthinus (LXI. 91);

and to other flowers:

> ore floridulo nitens
> *alba* parthenice velut
> *luteumce* papaver (LXI. 198).

> floridis velut enitens
> Myrtus Asia ramulis
> quos Amadryades deae
> ludicrum sibi roscido
> nutriunt humore (LXI. 21);

Catullus compares himself to a flower crushed by the plough:

> nec meum respectet, ut ante, amorem,
> qui illius culpa cecidit velut prati
> ultimi flos, praetereunte postquam
> tactus aratro est (XI. 21).

Metaphorically are found, *flos* (XVII. 14; LXIII 64; C. 2); *flosculus* (XXIV. 1); *florens* (LXIV. 251); *floridus* (LXVIII. 16); *floridulus* (LXI. 198).

From the farm come two metaphors:

> non si densior aridis aristis
> sit nostrae seges osculationis (XLVIII. 5);

> namque velut densas praecerpens cultor aristas
> sole sub ardenti *flaventia* demetit arva (LXIV. 353);

so Achilles mows down the ranks of Trojans.

Troubles are "thorny:" *spinosas curas* (LXIV. 72).

Apart from their use in figures, plants and flowers are of little interest. Cyrene is *Lasarpicifer* (VII. 4), Cytorus *buxifer* (IV. 13). There are the olive (XXXIV. 8; ash XVII. 18), myrtle (LXI. 22); ivy (LXI. 34). To the wedding of Peleus and Thetis Penios brings

> altas
> fagos ac *recto proceras stipite* laurus,
> non sine *nutanti* platano *lentaque* sorore
> flammati Phaethontis et *aerea* cupressu (LXIV. 288)

and Chiron

silvestria dona:
nam quodcumque ferunt campi, quos Thessala magnis
montibus ora creat, quos propter fluminis undas
aura parit flores tepidi fecunda Favoni,
hos indistinctis plexos tulit ipse corollis,
quo permulsa domus iocundo risit odore (LXIV. 279).

Attis' door is decorated *floridis corollis* (LXIII. 66), and
Hymen is bidden

cinge tempora floribus
suave olentis amaraci (LXI. 6).

Animals   Animals are of little interest. Catullus compares his songs for his brother's death to those
of the nightingale:

qualia sub densis ramorum concinit umbris
Daulias, absumptei fata gemens Itylei (LXV. 13).

Doves are typical of conjugal happiness:

nec tantum niveo gavisa est ulta columbo
compar (LXVIII. 127).

The sparrow of Lesbia (II; III) is interesting to Catullus
solely for its mistress' sake. The crow and vulture appear
as birds of prey (CVIII. 4), and beasts and birds of prey
appear again in LXIV. 152.

The spider's web is symbolic of worthlessness:

plenus sacculus est aranearum (XIII. 8).

and of oblivion:

nec tenuem texens sublimis aranea telam
in deserto Alli nomine opus faciat (LXVIII. 51).

The boar is *aper nemorivagus;* the deer *cerva silvicultrix*
(LXIII. 72). The deer is the type of swiftness:

nascetur vobis expers terroris Achilles

.   .   .   .

qui persaepe vago victor certamine cursus
flammea praevertet celeris vestigia cervae (LXIV. 338),

the lion of cruelty (LX. 1; LXIV. 154), and of fierceness:

> ni te perdite amo: ,
>
> .   .   .   .
>
> solus in Libia Indiaque tosta
> caesio veniam obvius leoni (XLV. 3).

Ululatus is used figuratively of shouting (LXIII. 24; 28). Other animals are the goat (figuratively XVII. 15), the mule (XVII. 26), cattle, to symbolize subjugation:

> veluti iuvenca vitans onus indomita iugi (LXIII. 33).

also LXVIII. 120.   The attendants of Cybele are *Dindimenae dominae vaga pecora* (LXIII. 13), *Remugire* is used of the "tympanum" (LXIII. 29).   In connection with agriculture cattle appear in LXII. 49; LXII. 64; LXIV. 38; as victims in LXIV. 389.

The country is spoken of with contempt:

> idem infaceto est infacetior rure (XXII. 14).

Summary
" It is in comparison that Catullus' sentiment for nature is most evident " says Secretan [95] and this statement is abundantly supported by the foregoing quotations.   It is especially true of the sea and of plants and flowers.   Metaphors and symbolization from nature are also common.   Epithets are relatively very numerous and very varied.   Lucretius' work contains nearly five times as many verses as Catullus', but he uses less than twice as many epithets of nature, and as to variety, only about one-fourth more.   Of Catullus' epithets about three-fourths are used only once, and about one-quarter of the total number are used of the same form of nature by no other poet of our period.   Nature is generally described in her peaceful moods.   Only of the sea are commonly presented fierce and unfriendly aspects.

That Catullus speaks often of the immensity of the sea is true, but that he speaks less often of its stormy aspects, [96]

---

[95] *Du Sentiment de la Nature dans l'Antiquité Romaine*, p. 81.
[96] Secretan, p. 60.

a study of his epithets will disprove, though there is no long description of a storm. Even in the graceful picture of the Argo's voyage the element of danger is evidenced by the words *ausi sunt* (p. 192).

The pleasure of Catullus' own voyage in the phaselus seems concentrated in the home-coming, and the little boat is regarded with wonder as the survivor of the perils of the deep. So too in his lament at his brother's tomb, he tells of the *multa aequora* (CI. 1), over which he has passed, the underlying thought being of the long and tedious journey. And Attis, addressing his companions, expresses the same idea: "You have endured the restless brine and cruel sea " (LXIII. 16).

Yet, though these aspects of the sea are oftenest alluded to and expressed by the use of epithets, the stormless sea is not without representation.

In a word is brought before us the surf upon the coast, on the "foamy shores of Dia" (LXIV. 121), and the shore which "is beaten by the Eastern wave resounding far " (XI. 3). More elaboration of description is found in the account of Attis standing on "the wet (sands) of the foam-whitened beach," "near the bright level of the sea " (LXIII. 87), and still more elaborate is the picture, or succession of pictures, of the sea in the famous simile in the *Peleus and Thetis* (p. 192).

More than any other poet of the republican period, Catullus represented the sympathetic relation between man and nature. Continually throughout the *Attis* and the *Peleus and Thetis*, particularly the latter, the mood of the suffering human being, and thereby its influence upon the reader, is intensified by the character of the natural surroundings. The sea-shore and the sea enhance the loneliness of the scenes in the laments of Ariadne and of Attis. The latter turns toward his lost home and longs for it "looking upon the lonely sea with tearful eyes" (LXIII. 48). So too Ariadne, deserted by Theseus, climbs to the hilltop and thence "gazes upon the lonely waves of the sea" (LXIV. 127) and feels herself hopelessly abandoned, hemmed in by the waters (LXIV. 134), where "no mortal appears upon the empty seaweed" (LXIV. 163), and she stands by the lonely sea, and while its waves sweep up the beach, within her own heart great waves of sorrow roll (LXIV. 62). Catullus calls upon the waters of his lake to rejoice with him upon his return to Sirmio (XXXI. 13); and the stars are called on as witnesses of and perhaps sympathisers with the loves of men (VII. 7). The obverse of this feeling is brought out where Catullus contrasts the coming and going of the bright days (*soles*) with their short intermission of night, and his own brief season of happiness, to be followed by perpetual night (V. 4).

It is in the *Peleus and Thetis* that the largest proportion of the descriptions of nature is found, and that the traces of sympathetic conception of nature are most evident. And these seem to partake of the artificiality of the other portions of the poem. They lack the spontaneity that characterizes all phases of Catullus' shorter poems, and all references to nature in Lucretius, and though we have not Catullus' Alexandrian models, we may surmise that to them must partly be laid the use of nature characteristic of this poem. Had this attitude toward nature been purely natural to the Roman poet, he would surely have shown more of it in the briefer poems in which his own feelings are so strongly and freely expressed. But his interests were in man rather than nature, and it seems to be only under outside influence that he cares to use nature in any way to deepen and enhance the expression of feelings.

10. PUBLIUS TERENTIUS VARRO ATACINUS.[97]

Of the twenty-four fragments of Varro Atacinus, about
half treat of nature.   The most extensive references are
Sky   to the heavens and the heavenly bodies.   They
are to be found in the *Chorographia*, and are purely geo-
graphical or astronomical in their nature, the relative
positions of earth, stars, and sea being discussed (Varr.
At. *Chor.* I. II. III).   In the *Argonautica* is one mythological allusion to the sun,

> cum te flagranti deiectum fulmine, Phaethon (*Arg.* IV. I),

and another to its heat:

> quas solis valido nunquam vis atterat igne (*Chor. Pro.* III. IV),

and in the *Ephemeris*, clouds are compared to masses of
wool: *Nubes (ut) vellera lanae stabant (Eph.* I.).
There is one picture of the quiet and peace of night:

> desierant latrare canes urbesque silebant
> omnia noctis erant placida composta quiete (*Arg.* III. I).[98]

A ship is compared to a chariot:

> Tiphyn (at) aurigam celeris fecere carinae (*Arg.* I. III).

The connection of the following line,

> deinde ubi pellicuit dulcis levis unda saporis (*Bell. Scq.* II.).

is doubtful.
Plants   There is a scientific account of a certain reed
of India in the *Chorographia* (*Asia*) and a picture of the
trees in autumn:

> frigidus et silvis aquilo decussit honorem (*Arg.* II. III).

Animals   The fragments of the *Ephemeris*, a translation
of Aratus, are all concerned with nature.   Besides the one
already quoted, are two references to animals:

---

[97] References are to Riese's " *Varronis Saturarum Reliquiae*" 1865.
[98] Of winds is found only *frigidus aquilo* (*Arg.* II. III); of rivers only
the *Nile* (*Chorag. Africa*).

8

tum liceat pelagi volucres tardaeque paludis
cernere inexpleto studio certare lavandi
et velut insolitum pennis infundere rorem.
aut *arguta* lacus circumvolitavit hirundo (*Eph.* II.);

et bos suspiciens caelum (mirabile visu)
naribus aërium patulis decerpsit odorem
nec *tenuis* formica cavis non evehit ova (*Eph.* III.).[99]

Summary   The treatment of nature is on the whole uninteresting.   Most of the references are found in works which
deal with phases of nature scientifically, and they do not
rise above this character, except perhaps in the description of the silence of night, and in that of the birds, which
is a translation from Aratus.

---

[99] Cf. Serv. in Verg. Georg. I. 375.

CHAPTER III.

THE REPUBLICAN PERIOD AS A WHOLE.

Of all the forms of nature represented in the poetry of this period, the sea is most interesting. Many aspects are **Sea** shown, but the open sea is more conspicuous than the shore, the stormy sea than the calm. Ships are very often mentioned, but the only poet who seems to feel real pleasure and exhilaration in the free movement of the boat over the water is Ennius.

Of epithets applied to the sea those expressing the most obvious characteristics, saltness, *salsus*, and magnitude, *altus*, and *magnus*, are first in number. Next come those expressing color, of which the commonest is *caerulus*.

Figuratively the sea usually represents misfortune. Many figures are drawn from shipwreck, and human cares and trouble are often represented as waves. The sea is very commonly invested with life, and in these cases is almost always shown as the cruel enemy of man. From Livius' "Nothing worse tortures man than the savage sea" to Catullus' "threatening Adriatic," this aspect is prominent in almost every author, and the feeling toward the sea most often to be inferred is a sense of this power and cruelty, a feeling of dread and at the same time of the fascination which may accompany such dread.

Next to the sea in interest is the sky with its sun and stars. Epithets most commonly used of it are *altus*, *magnus*, **Sky** *caerulus* and *caeruleus*. Its apparent shape, too, is often shown. In the tragedies it is often identified with Jupiter, often addressed as if so identified. Awe and wonder seem to be the feelings most clearly shown in connec-

204 BULLETIN OF THE UNIVERSITY OF WISCONSIN.

tion with it. These are voiced most plainly by Lucretius. "Look up into the clear bright color of the sky and what it holds within itself, the constellations straying here and there, the moon and the brightness of the sun with its brilliant light: if all these unexpectedly and suddenly were now presented to mortals, what more marvellous than these could be told of?"

Sun The characteristics most noticeable are, naturally, its heat and light. The epithets most used of it express the latter, *candidus* being most common, *aureus*, *radiatus*, *flammeus* next.

Though seldom used in figures to illustrate other things, it is itself very often figuratively represented. It is frequently described by Lucretius as a fountain from which flow light and heat, but more often than in any other way it is depicted with the qualities of life and personality. This personalizing is often of the mythological type (almost always so in the tragedies), the sun being represented as *Phoebus*, *Hyperion*, etc. Even where this is not the case mythological personalization is implied in the method of representation, as "thou sun who dost lift aloft in the sky thy glowing torch" (Enn.), and "the sun with the glowing eyes of his golden face had scanned the bright air . . and put to flight the shades of night with his swift steeds of the ringing hoofs." (Cat.).

Moon The moon is seldom spoken of at all, and never with any fullness of description. She is usually represented in eclipse, or mythologically as Diana, Phoebe, etc; and in "thou moon who alone of the gods dost look upon the perjuries of man" (Incert. Baehrens).

The only epithets used are *clarus* (Cic.; Luc.); *candens*, (Varr.), *almus* (Laevius), *alba leni lactea luce* (Enn.). No feeling for the beauty of the moon or her light is anywhere shown unless in the last of these, though Lucretius mentions

her among the phenomena of the sky which call forth men's
admiration. Stars are most interesting as they are de-
Stars   scribed in the constellations (especially in Cicero's *Phaenomena*), and in the description of night personified, in the tragedies. "Night moves on decked with glittering stars" (Enn.), or of the night sky, "when the air
far and wide painted with glowing fires was showing forth
the starry host" (Varr.). The epithet most frequently
used by Cicero is *clarus*, by all writers in general *fervidus*,
fulgens, micans, splendidus. They are often invested with
life, when their movement in the heavens is described.

Clouds are important only in Lucretius who
Clouds   shows a deep interest in them from a scientific and probably from an aesthetic point of view as well.
Elsewhere they are described as the source of storm and
rain (Enn.; Varr.). They are compared to masses of
hanging wool by Lucretius and Varro Atacinus.

Dawn is shown sometimes in its aspect in the
Dawn   sky, as "now do I see dawn reddening in the
sky" (Acc.), but more commonly on the earth, as "the earth
was exhaling mist to the damp dawn" (Pac.). It is
definitely personified only in Incert. Trag.; Varro; Catullus.
Epithets are few, *umidus* taking first place. *Roseus* is
found in Lucretius.

Night is interesting only in the tragedies,
Night   where it is almost always very definitely
personified as "dark-haired Night, daughter of Erebus"
(Incert. Trag.). Usually night is a time of misfortune.
Very seldom its calm and peace seem to appeal to the
writer, as in Ennius,' "dead and in ashes they lay in the
calm night."

Winds often symbolize fickleness. Their
Wind   fierce aspect is commonly presented, and like
the sea, they are usually the enemy of man. Catullus is
the only poet who more often represents their friendly as-

pects. The commonest epithets are *validus, saevus, violens.*
By these epithets they are often personalized, and sometimes in more full descriptions, as "the wind began to puff
out its cheeks and apply the spurs" (Varr.), "now they
take breath, and grow in force, and as it were, rallying,
advance, and, beaten, retreat" (Luc.).

Seasons
The seasons are very meagerly represented.
Spring is the only one in which pleasure seems
to be expressed, though Lucretius speaks of the *variae
lepores* which return with the changing seasons.

Streams
Streams are used in similes with comparative frequency. Gushing springs and full-
flowing rivers are most commonly depicted, as "on the
summit of a high mountain a bright stream leaps from
the mossy stone and . . . rolls headlong down the
sloping valley" (Cat.) and "rivers flowing level with their
banks" (Luc.). The commonest epithet is *rapidus.* They
are seldom personalized. When they are, the mythological idea of a river god is apt to be prominent, as
in *sanctus Tiber* (Enn.).

Mountains
Mountains are almost always shown as rough,
dreary and cold, the home of wild beasts.
Even Ida, to which the epithet *viridis* is applied more often
than to other mountains, is shown under the same aspect;
"have I come to the woods of Ida to live amid the snow
and the cold lairs of wild beasts?" (Cat.). Few epithets
show any but the most obvious characteristics. The most
usual being *altus* and *magnus.*

Lucretius is the only exception to these statements.[1] In
him is seen, if not the modern passion for the mountains, at
least an awakening sense of their peaceful calm and picturesqueness.

---

[1] Fairclough, *The attitude of the Greek Tragedians toward Nature,*
finds many traces of the modern feeling in the Greek tragedians.

Woods Woods are represented in much the same way as mountains, indeed they are usually mentioned together. A different aspect is shown only in a few passages where they are called "the home of singing birds" (Luc.), and sometimes in the representation of individual trees, as in the wood cutter's scene in Ennius. In the last, and in the expression *comata silva* (Cat.), there is some degree of personalizaticn.

Plants Individual trees are most interesting in Ennius, other plants in Catullus. Catullus indeed, is the only poet who represents flowers further than by mere incidental mention. No other poet, with the exception of Lucretius and possibly Calvus, mentions them at all. No plants are described with any detail. The description of pines in Ennius, *nutantibu capitibus . . . procerae*, and Catullus, *corniger . . . sudanti cortice*, are as interesting as any.

Animals Animal life is fully represented by almost every poet. Of wild animals, the lion and the deer are most conspicuous. The latter is more picturesquely described as *bisulcis ungulis, silvaticus, volabilis* (Varr.), *alipes* and *corniger* (Luc.); *silvicultrix* and *celer* (Cat.). Domestic animals are more conspicuous than wild, and among them the horse is every where most important and described with most variety.

Omissions The common forms and aspects of nature least well represented, as shown above, are the calm sea, the moon, clouds and rainbow, mountains, woods and flowers. Though dawn and early morning are often described, a sunset sky is never spoken of. In general there is great lack of detail and the phenomena described are the most obvious only.

Figures Figures taken from nature are, on the whole, not of very great interest. Similes are found less frequently than metaphorical expressions, and are usually drawn from plants and animals.   The longest and most elaborate simile is taken from the sea, and is found in Catullus.

Figures drawn from nature very commonly illustrate human life, especially the abstract.   The fire of love is likened to a volcano in eruption (Cat.).   Anger is like a rushing stream (Naev.). Sadness is a mist (Pac.). Ignorance is darkness (Luc.).   Trouble of various sorts is likened to shipwreck (Incert. Trag.; Cat.); to darkness, (Luc.); to a steep path (Luc.); to waves (Cat.; Luc.); to briers (Lucil.; Cat.). A person in trouble is like a crushed flower (Cat.); help in trouble is a favoring wind to the shipwrecked sailor (Cat.); a stream to the thirsty traveller (Cat.).   Glory is evanescent like melting ice (Liv.); virtue grows green like a plant (Ant.); fickleness is likened to the wind (Luc.; Cat.); to a moving cloud (Cat.).

Analogies between nature and the concrete in human life are less often noted.   Flying spears are likened to rain (Enn.); to hail and snow (Pac.).   Battle is like meeting winds (Enn.), and Lucretius speaks of "waves of war." A ship moving over the water is a water-spider (Varr.); a bird (Ant.; Enn.; Laev.).   Crowds of men in flight are like a rushing stream (Varr.); increasing crowds like a roughening sea (Cat.).   The young girl is like a flower (Cat.). Analogies between the actions of men and animals are among those most commonly noted.

Analogies between different forms and phenomena of nature are less frequently noted than those between nature and man.   The sea is a meadow (Acc.; Enn.; Luc.).   Mist and the sky (Enn.; Luc.) are likened to the sea; thunder to the sound of waves (Luc.); the sun is a fountain (Luc.).

Least common of all figures where nature is concerned are those in which nature is illustrated from human life. A mountain is a wart (Incert. Trag.); mountains are columns (Acc.; Cat.). The stars in the sky are "spoils" (Varr.); leaves on trees are likened to hair (Cat.); and forests on mountainsides to the same (Luc.).

But the various forms of nature are very com-
Personaliza- monly invested with the characteristics of life.
tion In addition to what is implied in many epithets used, such expressions are found as *ululare* of the sea,
(Enn.); *latratus* of the sea (Acc.); *radere* of a stream (Acc.;
Luc.); *pascere* of the stars in the ether (Luc.). Very often
nature is given attributes not only of life, but of human
life. It may be merely the physical appearance or activities of human beings to which a likeness is seen, as in
such expressions as *cacchinare* of echo (Acc.); of waves
(Cat.); *tacere* of night (Cat.); *boere* of echoing hills (Pac.);
the waging of war by the winds (Luc.); *fremitus* of woods
(Enn.). Or emotions like those of human beings are
attributed to nature, as by such epithets as *avidus* of
mountains (Luc.), the verb *vesanire* (Cat.) of wind, and
especially by the language of many descriptions of the sea.

This personalization of nature may be either of a mythological character, as when the dawn is represented as Aurora[2] (Cat.); the sky as identical with Jupiter (Enn.); the
sea as Neptune (Enn.); the moon as Phoebe (Incert.), [3] and
Diana (Cat.); the Tiber (Enn.) and Scamander (Acc.) as
sanctus. The most frequent and interesting cases of this
sort of personalization are in the case of the sun and of
night in the tragedies, where they are very commonly
shown as traversing the sky in chariots aglow with fire and
decked with stars, respectively, and where the sun and the
sky are often called upon as if cognizant of and interested in
the affairs of men.

The last type of the personalization of nature to be noticed is that where nature is not only endowed with the
power of action like that of man and with emotions belonging to humanity, but is shown as in intimate, sympathetic,
and often reciprocal relations with man, not as god or
goddess, but in her own form through the inner spirit in-

---

[2] The mere use of the term *aurora* of course does not always imply that
personalization was felt.

[3] Baehrens.

fused into her by the human spirit. This attitude toward nature is very rarely shown at all, never fully developed. In the setting of a scene a trace of it is perhaps found once in Ennius (see p. 101), once perhaps in Accius (p. 114), several times in Catullus, in the *Peleus and Thetis* and the *Attis.* (p. 200).

Epithets   A few general conclusions as to the use of epithets for nature will be of interest. Epithets for plants and animals are not included except in special cases.

Different authors show considerable differences in the epithets used of the several forms of nature. *Altus*[4] of the sea seems to be the most general, *salsus*[5] and *magnus*[6], of the sea, next. Others used by three or more authors are *altus*,[7] of the sky; *screnus*,[8] of the sky; *ardens*,[9] *aureus*,[10] *candidus*,[11] *clarus*,[12] of the sun or its light; *fervidus*,[13] *fulgens*,[14] *micans*,[15] *splendidus*,[16] of the stars; *saevus*[17] of wind; *altus*,[18] *arduus*,[19] *asper*,[20] *celsus*,[21] of mountain regions; *caerulus*[22] or *caeruleus, canus*,[23] of the sea-foam.

[4] Liv.; Enn.; Pac.; Acc.; Incert. Trag.; Laev.; Cic.; Luc.; Cat.
[5] Enn.; Acc.; Lucil.; Porc. Lic.; Luc.; Cat.
[6] Liv.; Enn.; Lucil.; Carm. Marc.; Luc.; Cat.
[7] Acc.; Varr.; Luc.
[8] Enn.; Porc. Lic.; Luc.
[9] Acc.; Luc.; Cat.
[10] Enn.; Luc.; Cat.
[11] Enn.; Acc.; Incert. Trag.; Luc.; Cat.
[12] Cic.; Luc.; Cat.
[13] Cic.; Varr.; Luc.
[14] Enn.; Cic.; Luc.
[15] Cic.; Luc.; Cat.
[16] Enn.; Acc.; Luc.
[17] Pac.; Lucil.; Val. Aed.; Luc.; Cat.
[18] Liv.; Naev.; Luc.; Cat.
[19] Enn.; Pac.; Luc.
[20] Enn.; Pac.; Lucil.; Cic.
[21] Liv.; Acc.; Cic.
[22] Enn.; Cic.; Varr.: Luc.; Cat.
[23] Enn.; Cic.; Luc.; Cat.

Many epithets are used of certain forms of nature by one author only. Important among these are, of the sky, *albus* (Cat.); *altisonus* (Enn.); *aureus* (Varr.); *candens* (Enn.); *cavus* (Enn.); *clarus* (Luc.); *convexus* (Cic.); *inmoderatus* (Cic.); *lucidus* (Luc.); *profundus* (Enn.); *purus* (Luc.); *signifer* (Luc.); *sublimis* (Luc.); of the sun and its light *albus* (Enn.); *igneus* (Incert.); *laetus* (Cic.); *liquatus* (Cic.); *micans* (Acc.); *nitidus* (Cic.); *obstipus* (Enn.); *praeclarus* (Luc.); *radians* (Cat.); *rapidus* (Cat.); *roseus* (Luc.); *splendidus* (Luc.); of stars, *candidus* (Luc.); *conlucens* (Cic.); *fervens* (Cic.); *inlustris* (Cic.); *lucens* (Cic.); *serenus* (Luc.); *severus* (Luc.); *splendens* (Cic.); *volucer* (Cic.); of the moon, *albus* (Enn.); *almus* (Laev.); *clarus* (Cic.); *candens* (Varr.); *lacteus* (Enn.); *lenis* (Enn.); *roscidus* (Egnat.); of clouds: *aereus* (Cat.); *aetherius* (Luc.); *aqualus* (Varr.); *caeruleus* (Cic.); *flammeus* (Luc.) *furvus* (Luc.); *niger* (Luc.); *opacus* (Cic.); *splendidus* (Luc.); *umidus* (Enn.); *volans* (Luc.); of wind: *aereus* (Cat.); *altitonans* (*Volturnus*, Luc.); *ferus* (Luc.); *furens* Enn.); *horribilis* (Cic.); *imbricitor* (Enn.); *ingens* (Enn.); *magnus* (Luc.); *phreneticus* (north wind, Varr.); *rapidus* Luc.); *silvifragus* (Luc.); *vehemens* (Cic.); *ventosus* (Cat.); *violens* (Luc.); *volans* (Luc.); of the sea: *albus* (Varr.); *acerbus* (Luc.); *aquilus* (Varr.); *asper* (waves, Enn.); *avidus* (Luc.); *ferus* (Cat.); *flavus* (Enn.); *glaucus* (Luc.); *horridus* (Cat.); *horrisonus* (Cic.); *immanis* (Luc.); *immensus* (Luc.); *impotens* (Cat.); *infidus* (Luc.); *immisericors* (waves, Acc.); *importunus* (waves, Liv.); *inflatus* (Cic.); *minax* (Cat.); *mollis* (waves, Luc.); *naviger* (Luc.); *proclivus* (waves, Cat.); *ridens* (Luc.); *sonorus* (Luc.); *subdolus* (Luc.); *ventosus* (Cat.); *viridis* (Ant.); of streams: *amoenus* (Luc.); *candidus* (Enn.); *celer* (Naev.); *largus* (Luc.); *lubricus* (Luc.); *radens* (Luc.); *rapax* (Luc.); *validus* (Luc.); of mountains and mountain regions: *aereus* (Cat.); *avidus* (Luc.); *buxifer* (Cytorus, Cat.) *cavus* (Luc.); *confragus* (Naev.); *lauricomus* (Luc.); *obstipus* (Enn.); *opacus*, (of doubtful meaning, Luc.); *praeruptus* (Pac.); *scruposus* (Pac.).

Most epithets are used of one form of nature only. Used of more than one form are: [24] *aereus* of clouds (Cat.); of the mountains (Cat.); *aetherius*, used of the sun (Luc.); of clouds (Cat.); *altus* of the sky (p. 210); of clouds (Luc.); of the sea (p. 210); of trees (Enn.; Varr.); *asper* of waves (Enn.); of mountains (p. 210); *candens* of the sky (Enn.); of the sun (Enn.; Luc.); of sea-foam (Luc.; Cat.); of the moon (Varr.); *candidus* of the sun (p. 210); of stars (Luc.); of rivers (Enn.); *clarus* of the sun (p. 210); of stars (Cic.; Luc,); of a stream (Luc.); of woods (Cic.); *ferus* of winds (Cic.; Luc.); of the sea (Cat.); of woods (Cat); *flammeus* of the sun's heat (Pac.); of its brightness (Acc.; Cat.); *fulgens* of the sky (Luc.; Cat,); of stars (p. 210); *horridus* of the sea (Cat.); of mountains (Pac.); *ingens* of the sky (Enn.; Luc;) of constellations (Enn.); *liquidus* of the sky (Enn); of the sea (p. 210); of streams (Naev.); of bird-notes (Luc.); *lucidus* of the sky (Luc.); of stars (Luc.); *magnus* of the sky (Enn.); of constellations (Cic.); of winds (Luc,); of the sea (p. 210); of rivers (p. 210); of oak trees (Enn.); *obstipus* of light (Enn.) of mountains (Enn.); *opacus* of clouds (Cic.); of mountains (Luc.); of woods (Cat.); *praeclarus* of the sun (Luc.); of stars (Cic.; Q. Cic.); *rapidus* of the sun (Cat.); of the wind (Luc.; Cat.); of streams (Acc.; Luc.); *saevus* of the wind (p. 210); of the sea (p. 210); *serenus* of the sky and light (p. 210); of night (Enn.; Luc.); of the motion of sky and sea (Porc. Lic.); *splendidus* of the sun (Luc.); of clouds (Luc.); *tremulus* of light (Enn.); of a comet (Cic.); of the sea (Cat.); *umidus* of clouds (Enn.); of dawn (Pac.; Cic.); *vagus* of storm (Luc.); of the sun (Cat.); of wind (Cat.); *validus* of the sun (Varr. A.); of wind (Luc.); of streams (Luc.); *vastus* of the sky (Enn.); of the sea (Cic.; Cat.); *ventosus* of the wind (Cat.); of the sea (Cat.).

Epithets denoting form are very rare. They are: *anfractus* of the seashore (Acc. Luc.); of a stream (Varr.);

Form   *cavus* of the sky (Enn.), of mountains (Luc.); *convexus* of the sky (Cic.); *curvus* of the seashore (Acc.; Cic.); *incurvus* of the seashore (Luc.).

Epithets of color, in so far as number and variety are concerned, are common, but the scope of each is wide and **Color**   the meaning apt to be indefinite.   Often, too, a general word expressing brightness is used where a color-term would be expected.   Of all color-terms *albus* has the widest scope.   It is used of the sky (Cat.); of the sun (Enn.); of the moon (Enn.); of the grape-leaf (Lucil.); of hail (Varr.); of a calm sea (Varr.); of sea-foam (Luc.); of the flower parthenice (Cat.); the hedgehog (Varr.); while *albicare* is used of the foamy sea beach (Cat.); of the foaming stream (Varr.); *albicascere* of the moon (Cn. Mat.); *subdealbare* of frost (Varr.).   *Candidus* is used of the sun (p. 210); of stars (Luc.); of rivers (Enn.); of the neck of the goose (Lucil.); *candor* is used of the sky at dawn (Pac.); of the stars (Cic.); *canus* of snow (Luc.); of the foamy sea (p. 210); *candere* of the sky and light (Enn.); of the sea in foam (Luc. Cat.); *incandere* of foaming water (Cat.); *niveus* is used of the sea (Cic.); of the dove (Cat.); *Lacteus* of moonlight (Enn.); *caeruleus* and *caerulus* are used of the sky (p. 210); of the sea (p. 210); of cloud (Cic.); of fields (Enn.); of olive trees (Luc.); of the snake (Enn.); of the whale (Cic.).

Viridis, *viridans*, etc., are used of fields and plants generally, of the sea only once (Ant.); *glaucus* is used of the sea (Luc.); grape-leaf (Varr.). *Purpureus* is used of the morning light (Cat.); of the grape (Lucil.); of snakes (Acc.); *purpurare* of the sea roughened by wind (Ant.). *Roseus* is used of the sun's light (Luc.); of dawn (Luc.). *Ruber* is used of the glow of lightning on the sea (Enn.); *rubor* of the eyes of the wild boar (Acc.); *rutilus* of stars (Cic.); of the lion's mane (Cat.); *rutilare* of the dawn (Acc.); *ostrinus* of dawn (Varr.), *puniceus* of the arbutus

214   BULLETIN OF THE UNIVERSITY OF WISCONSIN.

(Luc.). *Aureus* is used of the sky (Varr.); of the sun (Enn.; Cat.); *flammeus* of cloud (Luc.); of a boar's eyes (Acc.), *luteus* of the poppy (Cat.); *flavens* of a harvest-field (Cat.); *flavus* of sea-foam (Enn.); *fulvus* of dust (Enn.); of the lion (Luc.); *furvus* of cloud (Luc.); *fuscus* of night (Incert. Trag.); of the crow (Cic.). *Niger* is used of a storm (Cat.); of night (Varr.); *nigror* of night (Pac.; Luc.); of a cloud (Pac.); *nigrere* of the darkening of the sky with cloud (Acc.); with night (Pac.); *ater* is used of mist (Ant.); of cloud, figuratively, (Luc.).

Changing color and combination of colors is rarely noted. The blue sea turning white with foam, (Enn.; Cat.; Luc.), is commonest. The sky darkening with cloud (Pac.; Acc.); the sea with wind (Ant.); the rainbow in the dark clouds (Luc.); gray olive-trees among the darker green (Luc.); the changing plumage of the dove and peacock are the most elaborate examples. The verb *pingere* or its compounds is used of the skins of beasts (Acc.); stars in the sky (Varr.); shells on a beach (Luc.).

Except in reference to the sounds made by animals, sound in nature is less often and less fully represented than color, either by epithet or in other ways. Leaving out of account the many references to thunder, the sound most often represented is that of the sea upon the beach or stirred by moving boats. The sound of wind is next in importance. There is one reference to the sound of rushing streams (Cat.); and of rain (Enn.); very few to the song of birds (Sueius; Varr.; Luc.), and bleating flocks (Incert.); more to echo and to the beating of horses' hoofs. *Sonipes* is used of the horse by Accius, Lucilius and a fragment of tragedy of doubtful authorship. In the case of words expressing sound much indefiniteness is found. *Murmur* is used of thunder (Luc.), of wind (Luc.), and of the sea (Pac.; Cic.); *fremitus* of thunder (Luc.), rain (Enn.), of boats upon the sea (Acc.), of falling trees (Enn.), of the voice of the lion (Luc.); *fremere* of boats on the sea (Enn.).

Odor   Odors in nature are described by Lucretius in some scientific explanations. Elsewhere they are referred to with interest only in a very general way, once by Lucretius in the description of the seasons (p. 155), and once by Catullus, in speaking of wreaths of flowers. (p. 197).

Limitations   That there are decided limitations in the forms and activities of nature represented, and also in the representation of form, color, sound and scent in nature, in the poetry of this period has been shown in the above.   Other limitations and omissions are also noticeable.   Very few localities are mentioned by name and what are found are usually Greek.   No mountain, stream, island or lake in Italy is celebrated with the exception of Catullus' Sirmio.   Different forms of nature are rarely combined into a picturesque whole.   If they are mentioned together it is in a succession of single pictures or actions, not grouped as one.

Mythological representation of nature is comparatively rare (see p. 209), while the sympathetic or sentimental conception of nature finds still less representation (see p. 209). Both Euripides[25] and the Alexandrian poets[26] show a comparatively full development of this modern feeling toward nature.   What traces there are of such feeling in Roman poetry are seen most clearly in the poets who most depended upon these Greek writers, Ennius and Catullus.

It seems clear then that this sort of feeling was foreign to the Roman character at this time, and that since Roman literature was in its beginnings artificial, and had even at its beginning all Greek literature of the best period to de-

---

[25] See Fairclough: *The Attitude of the Greek Tragedians toward Nature.*

[26] See Biese: *Die Entwicklung des Naturgefühls bei den Griechen.*

pend on, no increase of such feeling is to be expected until
changes in the national life shall allow or encourage it to
develop, in other words, that, within this well-defined
period, there will be found uniformity. With the advent
of imperial government, with the new fashions and ideas
that grew up with it, with the growing tendency to intro-
spection that reveals itself in the imperial literature, a
natural and inevitable change in the feeling for nature
may be looked for also; and then, if ever, will take root
that subjective view which Euripides and the Alexandrians
especially well represent in the Greek.

This sort of feeling, combining in itself the elements of
many other kinds of appreciation, gives rise to the keen-
est and highest pleasure that can be felt in
nature. But that the Roman poets show
little of it in this period does not imply
that to them nature was without charm of any sort.

Roman interest in nature

With characteristic reserve indeed, they rarely express
in words any sort of feeling of appreciation for the
beauty, the grandeur, the wonder or the subtle charm of
nature. The only expressions definitely denoting beauty
or agreeableness are *laetus* and similar words of plants and
fields (Enn.; Luc.); *suavis* of flowers (Luc.); *egregius* of
colors and scents (Luc.); *iocundus* of odors of flowers
(Cat.); *dulcis* of a field and of trees (Luc.); *blandus* of
spring (Varr.); *amoenus* of willow-glades (Enn.); a stream
and Mt. Helicon (Luc.),[27] *vario lepore* of the changing seasons (Luc.), *honorem silvae* of leaves (Varr. A.), *voluptas*
of the sun (Gn. Mat.). It is only indirectly through
other sorts of epithets, through the use of figures, through
the many incidental allusions to nature where not de-
manded by the subject, through the vividness of some of
the brief descriptions, that the degree and the type of
appreciation natural to the Roman is to be seen. It ought

---

[27] Of a city. R. Pac. 124.

perhaps to be characterized rather as an appreciative interest in nature than a real love for her. The relation of nature to man's interest, the utilitarian view, is conspicuous, the relation of the sea to shipping, of the land to harvests, of mountains to comfort and discomfort.

Nature in action rather than at rest is shown not only by Lucretius, but by the other poets of the period as well. There are seldom seen languid moods, dull colors or half-lights. Everything is set forth in the bright light of the sun and in full vigor of action. The glowing sky, the brilliant sun traversing the heavens or pouring light upon the earth, the surging sea and rivers, the growing plant, are found in abundance. The same tendency, too, is seen in the frequency with which animal life is represented, and in the great frequency with which many forms of nature are personalized, or at least invested with the characteristics of life. In this attitude of mind, this conception of the vital force of nature, the Roman poet of this period was near one phase of modern nature-sentiment; the highest and most spiritual type of modern feeling he did not attain.

BIBLIOGRAPHY OF PRINCIPAL LITERATURE CONSULTED.

Baehrens, A.: Fragmenta Poetarum Romanorum. Leipzig, 1886.

Ribbeck, O.: Römische Tragödie im Zeitalter der Republik. Leipzig, 1875.

Mueller, L.: Q. Enni Carminum Reliquiae. St. Petersburg, 1884.

Mueller, C. F. W.: Ed. of Cic.; Vol. IV. 3. Leipzig, 1879.

Baehrens: Poetae Latini Minores. Leipzig, 1879.

Riese, A.: M. Terenti Varronis Saturarum Menippearum Reliquiae. Leipzig, 1865.

Buecheler, F.: Varronis Menippearum Reliquiae, in ed. of Petronius. Berlin, 1895.

Munro, H. A. J.: Lucretius. Cambridge, 1893.

Brieger, A.: Lucretius. Leipzig, 1894.

Heinze, R.: Lucretius, Book III. Leipzig, 1897.

Ellis, R.: Catullus. Oxford, 1878.

Sellar, W. Y.: Roman Poets of the Republic. Oxford, 1881.

Sellar, W. Y.: Roman Poets of the Augustan Age, Virgil. Oxford, 1883.

Schiller: Über naive und sentimentalische Dichtung. Written in 1795.

Humboldt, A. von: Kosmos, Vol. II. 1844.

Motz, H.: Über die Empfindung der Naturschönheit bei den Alten. Liepzig, 1865.

Secretan, E.: Du Sentiment de la Nature dans l' Antiquité Romaine. Lausanne, 1865.

Lübker, F.: Die Naturanschauungen der Alten. Flensburg. Prog. 1867.

ermann, K.: Über den Landschaftlichen Natursinn der Griechen und Römer. München, 1871.

edländer, L.: Darstellungen aus der Sittengeschichte Roms. Leipzig, 1888-90.

edländer, L.: Die Entstehung und Entwicklung des Gefühls für das Romantische in der Natur. Leipzig, 1873.

se, A.: Die Entwicklung des Naturgefühls bei den Griechen (1882), Römern (1884), im Mittelalter und in der Neuzeit (1888). Leipzig.

ss, E.: Die Natur in der Dichtung des Horaz. Düsseldorf, 1889.

umer, S.: Die Metapher bei Lucrez. Erlangen, 1893.

tcher, S. H.: Some Aspects of Greek Genius. London, 1893.

Laughlin, E. T.: Studies in Mediaeval Life and Literature. New York, 1894.

ynolds, Myra: The Treatment of Nature in English Poetry between Pope and Wordsworth. Chicago, 1896.

lgrave, F. T.: Landscape in poetry from Homer to Tennyson. London, 1897.

hns, L. O.: Treatment of Nature in Dante's Divina Comedia. London, 1897.

irclough, H. R.: The Attitude of the Greek Tragedians toward Nature. Toronto, 1897.

www.ingramcontent.com/pod-product-compliance
Lightning Source LLC
Chambersburg PA
CBHW030610270326
41927CB00007B/1118